Grace, Gaia,
and the
End of Days

Other Hay House Titles by Stuart Wilde

Books

Affirmations
The Art of Redemption
The Force
Infinite Self: 33 Steps to Reclaiming Your Inner Power
"Life Was Never Meant to Be a Struggle"
The Little Money Bible: The Ten Laws of Abundance
Miracles
The Quickening
The Secrets of Life
Silent Power
Sixth Sense: Including the Secrets of the Etheric Subtle Body
The Three Keys to Self-Empowerment
The Trick to Money Is Having Some!
Weight Loss for the Mind
Whispering Winds of Change: Perceptions of a New World

Audio Programs

The Art of Meditation
The Force (audio book)
Happiness Is Your Destiny
Intuition
"Life Was Never Meant to Be a Struggle" (audio book)
The Little Money Bible: The Ten Laws of Abundance (audio book)
Loving Relationships
Miracles (audio book)
Silent Power (audio book)

All of the above are available at your
local bookstore, or may be ordered by visiting:

Hay House USA: **www.hayhouse.com**®
Hay House Australia: **www.hayhouse.com.au**
Hay House UK: **www.hayhouse.co.uk**
Hay House South Africa: **www.hayhouse.co.za**
Hay House India: **www.hayhouse.co.in**

Grace, Gaia,

and the
End of Days

An Alternative Way for the Advanced Soul

STUART WILDE

HAY HOUSE, INC.
Carlsbad, California • New York City
London • Sydney • Johannesburg
Vancouver • Hong Kong • New Delhi

Published and distributed in the United States by: Hay House, Inc.:
www.hayhouse.com • **Published and distributed in Australia by:** Hay
House Australia Pty. Ltd.: www.hayhouse.com.au • **Published and
distributed in the United Kingdom by:** Hay House UK, Ltd.: www.
hayhouse.co.uk • **Published and distributed in the Republic of South
Africa by:** Hay House SA (Pty), Ltd.: www.hayhouse.co.za • **Distributed
in Canada by:** Raincoast: www.raincoast.com • **Published in India by:**
Hay House Publishers India: www.hayhouse.co.in

Editorial supervision: Jill Kramer • *Design:* Tricia Breidenthal

Interior illustrations and the Appendix article "The Matrix and the
Human Soul" reproduced by permission of Khris Krepcik.

Library of Congress Cataloging-in-Publication Data

Wilde, Stuart
  Grace, gaia, and the end of days : an alternative way for the
advanced soul / Stuart Wilde. -- 1st ed.
      p. cm.
  ISBN 978-1-4019-2006-7 (tradepaper : alk. paper) 1. Spirituality--
Miscellanea. 2. Spiritual life--Miscellanea. 3. Occultism. I. Title.
  BL624.W538 2009
  131--dc22   2008030550

ISBN: 978-1-4019-2006-7

12 11 10 09   4 3 2 1
1st edition, March 2009

Printed in the United States of America

Much love and many thanks to Udita Chohan and Khris Krepcik for their technical assistance with the information in this book and also to Suet Thow for her kind help in editing. And additional thanks to Khris Krepcik for his graphics.

CONTENTS

GRACE, HOPE, AND GOOD FORTUNE

1

The divine wind of grace offers you hope and good fortune—it can cure everything. It can grant you an invisible protection, a miraculous healing; it can offer you visions through what I call "pure information," which is downloaded data that comes to you directly as visions, extrasensory perception, and dreams. Grace can carry you to dimensions and places of learning far beyond anything discovered by humankind before. Grace can grant you clemency for your darkness and liberate you. Grace is pure love; it is a great gift, the Sacred Healer, but it is one that is poorly understood. In this book, I seek to redress that and give you the keys to levels of metaphysical comprehension and sophistication not available elsewhere.

To a Christian, grace is good fortune: it was an "amazing grace . . . that saved a wretch like me," as it says in the famous song. To a Hindu, it is good karma, enjoyed as beneficial events that flow to a pure soul. A Muslim might see it as the approval of Allah.

What *I* discovered is that grace is an energy, a technology from other dimensions that you can learn to harness and develop, and you can even watch it moving and flowing right here in 3-D. I don't mean this in an airy-fairy, "living in the light" New Age way. It is a real technology: a methodology of data transfer that's described in digital-fractal codes that arm you with a new power, a new discipline, a healing, and a protection that you can learn to acquire.

The Catholics talk of the "Virgin Mary, full of grace," but no one seems to have ever met one—those types of girls are rare down at the Dog and Duck pub where I hang out. And because the overall concept of grace got captured by religion, modern people tend to ignore it as irrelevant.

There is a mirror-world to ours where your mirror-self exists. The South American shamans call it the *Aluna,* a nice word meaning "of the moon." There are vast amounts of energy flowing out of the Aluna into our three-dimensional plane—more than all the power/energy consumed on Earth each day. But the airy-fairy context in which grace is set in today's mind is really a con-trip to make sure you ignore it.

We know so much about it now that was not known five years ago. It can heal you almost instantly, it can show you the other dimensions, and it can help protect you. It is vastly complex and laced with vital information and much love.

If I make it more technical, will you agree to believe in it more? It might save your life. It's a mathematical formula of pure love that's very ancient, far older than this universe. It is an overlay from a multidimensional hyperspace stated as an iteration of that ancient formula expressed as a binary on-off code, delivered (housed) in a digital-fractal geometry of great beauty and great complexity, like a fractal. If you're not familiar with fractals, you might like to look up the Mandelbrot set—it's the famous fractal that looks like a Buddha lying down on his side.

In the hyperspace of the inner worlds, information is housed in these geometric patterns—pictures of great complexity—just like pixels make up a digital photograph. The information flows from a place or places (dimensions) in colored tubes; and it rotates down from a 26-dimensional reality, through a 9-dimensional reality, down to us in 3-D. Opposite those 26 dimensions are thought to be 26 more in a further mirror-state, making 52 worlds, and the square of those is $52 \times 52 = 2,704$. So it is possible that grace is housed and delivered from a mega-gigantic artifact, vastly bigger than the universe that expresses or is laced in 2,704 dimensions. We don't know exactly, as it is too large for us to comprehend.

We know for a fact that the digital-fractal geometry of grace is a heavily data-laden supplement of great complexity—data your etheric (life force) understands and reacts to, even if your waking mind doesn't understand it. We can't as yet crack open one pixel of the data download in these fractal deliveries, as they move too fast. But when they are expressed in large numbers, we can easily feel them or even watch them in our mind's eye, so we know how to describe it all.

In simple terms, we say it is molecules of the Great Goodness, but it is vastly more complicated than that. Imagine that you're watching a man throwing seeds of wheat onto the ground in a field, and you're too far away to see any individual seed, but you can see a handful of them as a waveform tumbling on the ground. Now let's say that you've never seen wheat, and you don't know that the end result is a piece of toast for breakfast—grace is watched in the same way as a digital-fractal waveform that can produce endlessly varied results: some of it we understand and most of it we don't.

For example, in the power of grace there is a type of flutter that you first imagine as a fault in your nervous system, but it is in fact your etheric life force that's fluttering, so it's a quickening that you sense. The flutter sends data to your human cells instructing them to oscillate faster and become more alive. Essentially, the flutter is asking your cells to go backward in time biologically.

All the people I teach who get the flutter and any one of the other hundred or so artifacts (sensations of grace) start to look very alive and young for their age. It takes about six months for that change to be noticeable in people. They also develop superhuman stamina and strength, often sleeping just an hour or two a night. I can show you these things if you like, and I can tell you how to induce them, but the only thing I *can't* guarantee is that you'll see it all immediately. People's abilities differ. What is possible now is extraordinary.

The Peruvian-American writer Carlos Castaneda knew of these things. He was an extraordinary man much maligned and attacked in his life. He wrote of the shamans in the sparse lands in the north of Mexico. He isn't with us anymore, but strangely, he has no grave and no death certificate. He wrote in his books: "The warrior leaves no bones." He knew the secret. He knew of the song of the wind and the eagle's gift and the reality of the other worlds, describing them in a unique way. He had symmetry, and we now know he walked out of here—he did not die. We have always known that this type of walkout is possible, and Castaneda did it.

The parallel worlds are as close as the end of your arm, and I can show you more of this later. To do a

"Castaneda," you have to find the "Shimmering Door," a 26-dimensional portal, which is discussed in detail in a later section.

I hope you'll find this book at the very cutting edge of what humans know so far. To understand it and get the most out of it, you'll need an open mind, and then you'll have the understanding that almost everything you've read here is real. The dimensions are real; the otherworld sensations, like the flutter, are real; the celestial is real, as is the demonic. The inner beings are real, Kali is real, devils are real, angels are real, and all those subtle feelings and impressions you get and the visions and dreams and promptings you've had are real.

It wasn't always like this. It all changed a few years ago. In this book are many things you should incorporate into your life to increase your power, but it takes an intrinsic alignment in your feelings for real success. If you just skim-read this text with your mind, you'll miss the best of it, and your progress may be disappointing. You have to jump in "sight unseen," holding your nose and learn to trust.

Believe everything—that was *my* tactic . . . it worked brilliantly. The celestial all came true in the end, nothing went missing, and nothing in the complexity of the grace-data ever turned out wrong or misaligned. In years of watching it, we never made any real mistakes. Then again, there are many things we still don't know.

Do this first: hold your first two fingers up to the light, very close together, and you will see little black lines between them. If you can't see this, your fingers could be too wide apart or too firmly together. Those black lines are interference patterns that are created while particles of light (photons) are trying to squeeze between your fingers.

5

A very famous experiment was performed by Alain Aspect at the University of Paris in 1982 using those interference patterns to establish the nonlocal nature of the quantum world. *Nonlocal* means that things can be in two places at once. *You* are also in two places at once; there's another version of you, a mirror-self, an exact replica—the German word is *doppelgänger.*

In March 2001, 15 others and I experienced another form of interference pattern that we came to call the *Morph.* It looks like dry rain when it pervades the room, and there are swirls and patterns and speckled lights in it. When you put your hand up into it, your hand dematerializes from the tips of your fingers downward.

I wrote about the day that it first appeared in my last book, *The Art of Redemption.* Fifteen of us dematerialized in a house in Australia . . . but I won't go into that story here now, as the regular Stuie Wilde readers might get irritated reading it all again, so I've put the "Arrival of the Morph" story at the back in the Appendix for those new readers who haven't read it before and wish to do so now.

The Morph, as we understand it, is a 9-dimensional energy, which is actually part of a 26-dimensional world that threaded its way into our 3-D one. As it came into our world, it created the same interference patterns as those you see between your fingers, a 9-D light crossing our 3-D light, the difference being that the patterns of the Morph are vastly more complicated because it has trillions of quanta of information in it.

We found we could lie on a bed in meditation and download hundreds of four-color visions per day. I taught several thousand people to see it, and the Morph became our teacher. We compared information, and what one saw was what the others saw. It was uniform. It all comes from the same place.

I've jotted down more than 100,000 visions since it started eight years ago. I've seen many, many video clips—instructional videos that play in my mind's eye like watching TV—and some of them have played on an external wall of the room I was in, as if projected in the way a regular film might be.

Many of us have seen the honeycomb-patterned dome that surrounds us, which we call the *Matrix*. One day we broke through it, and beyond it is the mirror-world that the shamans of South America call the *Aluna*. Once the net of the Matrix was broken, our knowledge—which was already expanding by leaps and bounds—rocketed.

The story of how we broke the Matrix and got through was a big party and too long to tell here. The ghouls infest the Matrix as a control trip, so naturally they were trying to stop us, but we had help, and the Morph showed us how not to be scared of them any-more and how to beat them at their own game.

Anyone can get to the Aluna now through the Matrix. When you first see the Aluna, it looks like a blue-gray mist. Sometimes it has speckles in it, so that's why I named it "the speckled ambience."

Okay, let's move to the mother lode, lickety-split . . . good, good, good.

GRACE AND REINCARNATION 2

Humans aren't free. We're subjected to endless control and misinformation . . . it's a form of punishment. I don't know if you believe in reincarnation or not; if you don't, never mind—just come with me for now, if you will. I never really believed in it either, but we discovered in the Morph that reincarnation is real. Millions of humans have had lives here before; then again, billions are in their first one on Earth, and many have had incarnations in nonhuman dimensions. Interesting? Hard to fathom, eh?

A few New Age teachers write about reincarnation and past lives, but I'm sorry to say I was never very convinced, as what they taught seemed more about ego-rubs than facts. The Ayahuasca shamans of South America whom I've met admit that there's very little about reincarnation in the Ayahuasca worlds. The Buddhist teaching of a thousand lives on the wheel of fortune and misfortune seems a bit extreme and highly unlikely, just from a mathematical standpoint, since we don't have the global population for everyone to live a thousand lives. The Hindu teaching strikes me as more accurate, but the socioreligious idea of uppity Brahmans and lowly

9

untouchables seems rather unfortunate, and the notion of incarnating back as a dog or a flea seems doubtful.

On my first Ayahuasca journey, I asked about reincarnation and was told that "it is everywhere." Then, as I explained in a previous book, I asked to see God and was taken out into space; and God turned out to be a vast, orange elliptical shape, like an NFL football. The orange dots were all the human emotions and prayers pleading for help sent in that direction. The cloud of dots was quite diffused, kind of hovering listlessly in space like lost mail—undelivered parcels of energy—and I could see planet Earth through it far in the distance. I found God rather boring and vastly disappointing.

A long time passed, and then on my 34th Aya journey, two beings arrived at my side that I called "Purple and Blue," as those were the colors each radiated. They talked to me for four hours about the dimensions of Camelot, my life and my journey, my death, and certain key people I was thinking about at the time. Periodically they said, "Please, ask your questions."

I was so blown away by what they were telling me that I didn't *have* any to ask, and anyway, my brain wasn't functioning normally, as I was deep into my journey. Finally, embarrassed that I had no questions, I said, "Please tell me about reincarnation. What is real and true, and what is false?"

They said, "Do you think you are ready to know about reincarnation?"

To which I answered, "I think so." They agreed to take me.

Next, I found myself moving backward through many inner-space dimensions very quickly—so fast, in fact, that I had little time to comprehend what I saw to either side of me. Then I slowed down a bit, and I came upon a dimension of very beautiful geometries: vast oblong boxes, various shapes, and delicate lines. It was all in the distance, and I realized that this was where reincarnation was settled—for the time being, anyway— as far as my perspective was concerned.

As I got closer, I began to feel the pain of it: billions of women in labor (it was really quite disturbing) . . . and then I could feel the suffering of people's deaths, sickness, the wounds of war, accidents, drowning, murder, and so forth. The agony of cold, lonely deaths mixed with the pain of the human births was a great shock; and then when I saw the pain of all the human evil that reincarnation requires people to try to sort out, it overwhelmed me very quickly. The cycle of birth and death is all to do with evil. If people weren't arrogant and evil, they wouldn't have to incarnate here.

Incarnation is a gift, like a second chance for the hopelessly lost, but it's not the great wonderment of evolution that we think it is. That's an idea the ego thought up to make the need for itself reasonable and important. Yes, there are lessons to be learned by being a human, but they aren't ones that any decent spirit needs.

This is a correctional facility. With a few exceptions, people who don't commit crimes don't get sent here. Then again, some spirits must incarnate for other reasons—to experience Gaia (the self-correcting intelligence of the planet) in its natural, solid beauty; to serve; to help a family member from a past life make it; and a host of other reasons—but mostly it is all to do with ugliness, agony, and pain.

I later discovered that evil people die in agony and lose their faculties not because of crime and punishment, but because they fall victim to the ghouls (dark entities) that respond to the same ghoulishness in the sick humans. People walk around with their devilish attachments inches from their skin or in their bellies. Sometimes those attachments (entities) feed off them and eventually kill them, like a virus might. A virus is just an extension of one or more of the ghouls that created it. Without the ghouls, there would be no viruses.

I saw in the Aluna a famous teacher who is very rich. He had 160 ghouls in him or within a few feet of him. It was extraordinary; they hover close as he goes about his work. He is famous for overcharging people and gouging them. I had a little laugh when I said to myself, *So this is what the gods of overcharging look like.* They weren't very pretty.

I saw how the man will collapse soon, a victim of his rapacious greed, his need to be important. He seems to have a serious disease that can't be cured. I didn't see his previous incarnations, but he must have been an evil tyrant who fed off others, I imagine. Now he's strutting about in his squeaky-white act pretending to fix people. I'm sure he thinks himself a saint. Our delusions of grandeur are so disturbing to watch.

I discovered in the Morph worlds that many humans only incarnate here once, as their next incarnations aren't physical; many do so up to five times, and usually there's no need for more. The reason, as far as I can work it out, is that either people pull out of evil and the hell of this world or they drift ever lower to where they become so ghoulish that they're irretrievable, so after death they can't get out of the hells they descended into while alive.

Now I'm not talking about people like Hitler here, but rather about ordinary individuals like the teacher I mentioned—people who think they're normal. Ones you meet on planes, say, who might seem pleasant and reasonable when you first speak to them, until you discover their silent disdain and hatred and the hidden secrets of their lives.

Remember (I've said this before in my writings), only about 6 percent of people in the Western world are warm and normal, people who have a soul. The rest have no soul: they are devils, often in disguise—cold, cruel, cerebral, and arrogant. Lawyers, politicians, preachers, gangbangers, stockbrokers, the sellers of pyramid schemes, flimflam merchants, real estate agents, prolific consumers, the killers of animals, black magicians who don't realize they're black magicians—or *real* black magicians—or predators that spread fear and darkness for the thrill of it or to elevate themselves . . . human devils pretending to be normal.

Feeling the pain of billions of births was pure agony; and all the billions of lonely, painful deaths really scared me. The evil of humans and their incarnations and reincarnations was too much karma in motion for me to take—although watching it only took a few seconds, it was enough to make me violently ill and shudder with revulsion.

I said to the beings, "Please get me out of here. I didn't realize reincarnation was just the sum total of pain and evil and the failure to transmute it. It is making me very sick indeed."

The words had no sooner tumbled from my lips than I was gone, rescued by some benevolent force I couldn't see. I was really rattled, and it took me half an hour to recover. I can see now why reincarnation is kept a big secret from humans: it is all too depraved and disgusting to contemplate, and it would really scare people if they knew chapter and verse in advance. You don't get many chances, and this may be your very last. This is a correctional facility—if you remember that, it should spur you on a bit.

Yes, and the punishment here at the correctional facility called Earth is ignorance, pain, disease, and the presence of a billion ghouls you can't normally see that will make you sick and carry you toward despair and emotional turbulence. Then there are their assistants (allies): the dark and dangerous people the ghouls have secretly abducted and influenced, as well as the system that's stacked against you commercially and socially. At some point in history, "you did the crime, so now you have to do the time."

But the biggest punishment is the vast amounts of misinformation we're subjected to—information that's designed to keep us prisoners, sending us the wrong way and leading us into the arms of the ghouls and on to the gates of hell.

Most misinformation is backward in order to lead you the wrong way; or you misinterpret correct information, misaligning it, altering it in your mind. If people hear voices in their heads, it's symptom of mental illness or insanity, yet we humans constantly listen to a very dogmatic voice within—our own! Why we don't see *that* as a form of insanity is a bit of a mystery.

The churning of the mind is a disease. It takes you away from grace toward perdition. Discipline is the only way to enter the Tao and control the mind, and then you will get a proper perception that will allow you to understand the utter simplicity and power of grace and the complication and error in a lack of it. Dogma is part of our rotten karma; it leads people astray.

Inner blindness is another major setback; information blindness is an unfortunate karma that foils many an escape attempt. We can't normally see the inner worlds, as we are too surrounded by darkness—our own and the dark forces that respond to it—and of course, dark humans, of which there are hundreds of millions, maybe billions.

Here's something I was taught in the Aluna that's very revealing. When you close your eyes, you see darkness; certainly a little light can flicker in through your eyelids from the sun or a lamp, say, but essentially it's the dark that you see. But imagine if you were one of those rare humans who are multidimensional and very warm and celestial in their feeling: they also initially see darkness when closing their eyes, but after a few seconds, it adjusts and a celestial light appears and pours into them as grace, and they see inner worlds of great beauty and radiant colors.

In other words, the darkness you see when you close your eyes is a manifestation of your own darkness (your unprocessed shadow) within, and that comes from the ghoulish forces surrounding you in the dimension or mind-set that you live in—that you are in right now—as each ghoul blocks your inner light a little bit. So if you're wondering whether you've arrived to be heralded as a great Spirit Being, you only have to close your eyes to discover that you probably haven't—terrible stuff, so disheartening for the ego. However, if you close your eyes and see a blue-gray mist, that is the light of the Aluna. Between its dots will be the blackness of the ghouls, but sight of the mist is great progress even if what you see is very faint.

You may wonder why you haven't arrived as yet. Maybe you were genuine, but your karma didn't allow for it yet. Perhaps you, sadly, never had any decent information (*pure* information). And you were probably raised by dysfunctional, egocentric people who taught you to be like them, so they cut you off from grace; and sometimes that lack of the celestial light in your life made you scared, confused, and lonely. Sometimes the ghouls took advantage of that and tormented you, touching you invisibly via your etheric field with their pulses of evil, hoping to make you sick; or they infiltrated your dreams and nightmares, crept through your soul like snakes slithering toward a frail, blind, unsuspecting mouse.

The influence of that would have painted your soul in a patina of dark sentiments—silent rage, maybe, or thoughts of vengeance—or the pain of it all would have created in you a disdain for humanity and the animal world, and you might have learned to cut yourself off from people. Isolation is a manifestation of a silent hatred. Or, you became ever more the predator, controlling people and making them your slaves and victims, just as the ghouls silently control *you* in the dead of night to make you *their* victim. You mirrored what the ghouls secretly taught you and became like them—hellish.

Grace will cure that if you turn and go the other way. I'll show you. But you can't shake the ghouls overnight with a little "Shoo, shoo"—it doesn't work. There has to be a deep intrinsic realignment. You have to go wider to understand grace and to become safer. The world of the ego is vertical: it seeks altitude. The ivory tower of our self-importance that I wrote about in *The Art of Redemption* needs height; it needs one's nose in the air; it needs elitism, be it social or spiritual; it needs the elevation of specialness and the cold separation from humans who are considered lower. That is the ghouls' world. They abduct humans through importance.

If you've read my books, you'll probably know that I talk about the fact that light has a transverse wave that crosses the forward one at 90 degrees. Those transverse waves lead you to another dimension. The spiritual worlds are at 90 degrees to you. So I discovered that going wider and sideways, not upward, is the way to evolve. You ascend sideways—it sounds strange, doesn't it?

The wider you go, the more you see. Width comes from silence; humility; sacredness; reverence; prayer; and the Three Graces, which are tenderness, generosity, and respect. As you start to process your shadow and embrace grace, you develop "breadth of spirit": you become wider, and soon you become aware of many extraordinary facts about yourself.

Reincarnation is eternal, and some of it appears as if it's going backward in time. If you had a past life in the 1700s as a poet and before that as a Roman soldier at the time of Christ, say, those people are still alive in the Aluna worlds, and they exist simultaneously with this life of yours now. Humans are eternal, so it stands to reason that what you used to be must still be there in the spirit worlds, evolving someplace. That former human existence didn't just pop like a bubble-gum balloon might burst on your lips. They all still exist.

Now here is an idea that is jolly hard to get one's head around, but if you can grasp this, then you'll rocket forward. Imagine a Golden Radiant Being in an eternal hyperspace that stands 60 feet high and commands endless dimensions and universes and evolutions . . . that is, in effect, a god—one that exists and evolves in the company of other godlike beings of the same radiance. Then let's place that godlike being on the timeline marked below as GRB (Golden Radiant Being), as that's what you eventually became after thousand of eons had passed. That "future you" coexists with this current life—what you became eventually is already there in existence. You are behind it on a timeline, but it already exists.

Roman	Poet	You	GRB
soldier____17th c.	____now____(eternal)		

If you look at time as a straight line, the logic is hard to comprehend. Yes, one can imagine a human you used to be in a past life who's still evolving someplace concurrently with your life now—but how did the future radiant person come about, and how can he or she be in existence already if you haven't gotten there yet?

The answer I discovered arises from the fact that eternity has no future. There is only the eternal now and our past. So the trick to understanding it comes in bending the line. If you bend the line into a Möbius strip to describe eternity, you can see how all the lives and existences can be concurrent.

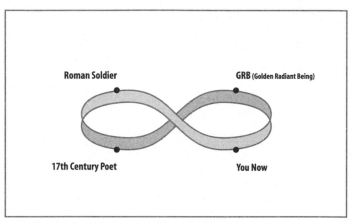

Fig. 1: The Möbius strip.

It doesn't matter where on the line you pick—you can never say which life is in front or behind the others; it all depends on where you start on the line and in which direction you choose to go. If you look at the strip from this side and you go around clockwise, that places the incarnations in a certain order, but what if you were on the other side of the strip through this page looking back at it? Then the incarnations would be in the opposite order.

So that's the backward-in-time element. And it goes way further than this, but we'll hold it here now so as not to lose the drift down the plug hole of confusion. Just remember this: what you became was/is a Radiant Golden Being. It all got resolved in the end.

GRACE AND YOUR SPIRITUAL LOGO

3

Inside you and around you is your spiritual logo, a digital-fractal set of symbols that describes the nature of the eternity of your soul, as well as the things you're aligned to in this lifetime. Forget your soul as a blob of light in your chest . . . that's for amateurs. Your soul can be vast—larger than a galaxy—but even if it's not vast as yet, it's often seen as a very large digital-fractal cube, the size of a small warehouse space. It's full of dynamic and fast-moving images: there are floating symbols/pictures of people you know today who are close to you, and your past lives hover in there as well, along with trillions of bytes of information about you and things that you're interested in now while alive.

That logo-cube hovering in its multidimensional hyperspace is dynamic and alive, changing minute by minute as your actions, feelings, and deep inner sentiments change. When you finally graduate from the Earth plane, that logo acts as your boarding card as you travel to your proper place in the celestial heavens . . . or you drift to the fractal hells . . . or you never get away from the Earth plane at all and remain earthbound to degrade into a demonic being, which I'll write about later in this book.

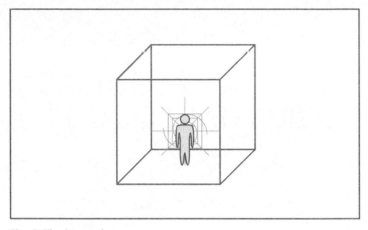

Fig. 2: The logo-cube.

I initially became aware of the logo-cube some years ago when it first appeared in my mind's eye. I was truly amazed by it. I hadn't known it existed, and I have since seen my logo six or seven times. There's always a multi-colored starburst in the middle; then lights and geometries go out from the starburst to the upper and lower corners of the cube, and it becomes larger and more defined and then begins to fill in with a multitude of colored patterns, events, people, and information.

Then playing cards appear: they seem to be holding hands, dancing next to each other, tumbling about—it is sweet to watch. (I used to teach blackjack years ago.) Then a very long curtain appears made up of letters of the alphabet because I'm a writer, and the letters dance and move and twist and turn, seemingly playing with each other, and that scene can go on for 20 minutes or more. I believe I was a painter many hundreds of years ago, and I see him floating through the logo every time, and all the while the logo gets prettier—and larger and larger.

I call it the "Tinkerbell Lounge," as it's so magical; and after a while, it evokes a feeling of safety and bliss as you're bathed in a molasses of color; and radiant hues wash you in the immediacy of it all. It's very intimate because essentially the Tinkerbell Lounge is sacred; it's the holy version of you.

Then things appear in the logo that I don't understand: formulas and plans and so forth that I think describe the modality of a "future me." I find those somewhat beyond my comprehension, so I just watch them without trying to work them out, and after maybe 40 minutes or so, the logo-cube fades and disappears. It's always slightly different when it comes back the next time—more is added. It's getting wider.

Each vision you have that comes as pure information to your mind is a gift, and that vision is added to your logo . . . or any information that comes as a feeling of knowing; an accurate prophetic dream; or an intuitive urge, maybe, to read a special book or to visit a certain place—it's all there in your logo. Nothing is lost, and it all adds to who you are: more and more beauty.

Now here is something unusual that we know from the Morph worlds: fine words and delicate prose that inspire you make the ghouls sick, as the sentiments evoked degrade the power of the demonic, as does an alignment with Gaia. So a walk in the woods when you're centered and balanced and happy starts to kill the ghouls around you. A sacred mantra uttered in reverence each day causes the same disastrous effect for them. Holy words from the Bible, the Koran, the teachings of Buddha, or beautiful poetry . . . they all help keep your logo ghoul free.

The fewer ghouls inhabit your life, the fewer physical difficulties you'll have. Most illnesses, except DNA malfunctions, are ghoul related. It is the darkness of these beings that are trying to make you sick (more on that later). We also know that if you remember any sacred invocations or beautiful prose, those words and their sentiments stay with you even after death, and they protect you in the afterlife.

Intrinsically you know how to make your logo beautiful; you know what is right, and you know if things in your life are ugly and what you have to work on. If you work hard, respect nature, and love Gaia and the Tao—and if you have love in your heart for all humans, even the evil ones—eventually a great gift descends upon you: the power to *see*.

Help arrives for you from the inner worlds. You're granted protection and power, and you're also given a silent perception that hasn't been seen here on Earth for 10,000 years or more, abilities greater than any humans who have ever lived since civilization began in 4000 B.C. But it's only for a while in this short age, and it's only if you remain silent and keep the power to yourself; you'll never be allowed to wield it or it will be snatched from you. Lust for power is a ghoul trait that will destroy you.

The Morph phenomenon I spoke of has taught us much over the years. It has allowed us to peer into other worlds: magical ones that seem to come from fairy books and others that are dark and demonic . . . we've seen both. There are higher beings—millions of them—that are close now because this is a critical time; we call it the "Renewal" because we see it as the time when Gaia takes back the earth and restores a new balance. That's why I call it the "End of Days," as it's the end of the old, ugly human days, but it's not the end of the world—just of our current one as we know it.

The Renewal is all part of a new dignity to be made manifest: the magical era of chivalry and the Scattered Camelots that I've written about before. It all became real in the end. I've found 30 Camelot anomalies around the world—doorways to another dimension—and there are 20 more I've never been to in Asia and the Caribbean and in remote icy places that I know about and don't care to visit. And there must be hundreds that I know nothing about.

Those doorways are open now or are about to open, and you can walk through, as Castaneda did. He wasn't the only one who has done it—I can give you a guarantee about that fact. How you get there is through the quality of your logo. But you can't work it out logically, hoping to find safety in an escape to the mountains; the celestial has to tell you where to go and what to do. It has to carry you because it loves you and because you have shown it evidence of true worth. The celestial protects itself from intruders.

To that end, the ghouls provide a useful function, as they torment dark people who seek to make the journey—the would-be travelers get very scared and quit. You can't get there if your darkness is still in place because you have to travel across a desolate inner plane to arrive, and you need a strong sense of self and a clean spirit or the ghouls will eat you. "Out there" is a very bare, ugly, and perilously open ground. If you're blind, with no inner sight, the ghouls will carry you off to their world, pretending that you're making it all the while.

The spiritual path is littered left and right with the souls of the failed and the damned. Very few avoid the pitfalls presented and make it in the end, but it *can* be done. It relies a lot on your humility, tenacity, and bravery, as well as your inner knowing—the kind that tells you to make a left when all logic and enticement says to go right.

We have learned to see, so we *know*—but that doesn't grant us a guarantee, as we have to remain pure and loyal to our ways. I've seen people arrive at the Camelot lake, Avalon, and then lose their place once more, drifting back to their darkness; the key to the door fell away. One day the Morph will dissolve and retreat once its task on Earth is completed. Humans aren't usually allowed to see, for our normal karma used to be to travel blind through the vagaries of mortal life. Things changed.

If you'd like to improve your logo right now, do this: Become extraordinarily polite when dealing with others; and never, ever veer from the soft gentility of politeness. Offer care and attention to everyone you meet, even if it is only for a few seconds—eyeball-to-eyeball attention is a form of love. In that politeness, you develop sensibility and tenderness; and flowers begin to grow in your logo, not the weeds of indifference, aggression, ego trips, and resentment.

It is a flick of the mind; be prepared to humble yourself, place your ego under others, and care for people by attending and being extraordinarily polite to them as a daily discipline in the accumulation of grace. A deep respect cleans your logo, and it heals it—it's important to remember that. Onward . . .

Dignity and graciousness describe the logo of a superior human, and as long as that dignity isn't expressed as pomposity or spiritual snobbery, then those qualities become your passport to a 26-dimensional place very few humans have ever reached. Only people of the elevation of Merlin and his partner, the lady Nimue, ever got there.

Dignity and grace describe a spiritual elegance that comes from inner knowing and strength and from having processed the dark shadow within you to arrive alongside the rivers of the Tao. From that elegance comes a natural silence and noninterference—the ability to move and act without anyone knowing, without causing a turbulence behind you; we say that it's the ability to walk through a wall without disturbing the bricks, without anything being touched or moved in any way. I don't mean this allegorically or hypothetically . . . I mean it literally. You're in a room, and you move to the next one, passing through the wall effortlessly.

Those superior humans stand straddled across an archway into their personal Camelot, so they have no need to change anything. While they may agree when asked to help others with their further knowledge or healing or their perceptions and understanding, they're also allowed to decline, for completed humans have no more debt to humanity. They are whole inside an imperfection that measures their ups and downs in life. They can serve if they wish, but they can also keep their perceptions to themselves if they so desire.

Just because you know something isn't necessarily a reason to talk about it. There are many things that others aren't ready to hear, or they're only ready to hear parts of it, not *all* of it. It's important to remember that. It's moving through life without disturbing things. Do you see the connection?

There are higher beings we have come to see through the Morph that we know and love. Their all-knowing is extraordinary to witness; it allows them to stand inside all things, but even in that heightened awareness, they still don't know everything, for their world is beyond vast—there are trillions of universes and endless dimensions. If the beings did know everything, their journey would be over, and the only way they could then go is backward toward degradation. They make mistakes and learn, just as we do.

Inside the dignity, beauty, and serenity of your logo—within the auspices of the eternal Tao and the Aluna—there is always the perpetual memory of your imperfection and darkness. That's why I say, "Don't struggle to be perfect; instead, work to become good." There's no way to wash away your sins, and no human can forgive them for you—that's a ghoul trick. All you can do is become so much light that your ancient failings are more or less irrelevant.

One night I saw a waterfall of thousands of small white pearls tumbling upon me . . . it was most delightful and mysterious and delicate beyond words. And yet to the right side of the waterfall of white pearls were three black ones, the memory of the record of my darkness. That vision describes exactly what I speak of here. Go to serenity and the Tao and it will carry you, and never mind what you did in the past as long as you've looked at it and understood it well and not denied it, and there is genuine contrition in your soul.

In one of the places where the attention of the higher beings exists, there are a series of golden orbs that hover in the air as an arch, each linked to another by a golden thread. When humans arrive and have resolved their darkness and understood the reality of the celestial, their faces appear reflected in one of the orbs. In this way I know which have arrived and which are still to come. I believe that eventually there are 600 adults in total I know who must come. This number isn't cast in stone;

it's just something that the mechanism inside me told me back in 1996. I presume it to be correct.

Every person in this group is unique in the sense that each has abilities and knowledge that the other 599 don't have. And while each may have a passing understanding of another person's celestial world or location, none has a complete understanding of *all* the different celestial worlds, as they don't have a complete belonging to everything. Then there are tens of thousands of people—maybe a hundred thousand—who will make it whom I'll never meet, for *I* am certainly not the prerequisite for all people's progress. I'm only the assistant to *some* people's progress, those few who needed me.

I'm like the ferryman who takes these lords and ladies across the river on their way to the Camelot castle . . . and I don't mean this allegorically—I mean it literally, insomuch as the Camelot castle is a way of describing your passage through the Shimmering Door to the worlds Castaneda arrived in. We know he commands more than one celestial dimension. Among his worlds is one of ice and snow, with the presence of many wolves. It is pristine, there is no sickness there, and the full moon lasts 28 days. In another, the people who arrived there like Castaneda did worship the sun, and the sunset in their world takes four hours. They dance and pray and celebrate at that time each day. It is most special for them.

There must be billions of these worlds—we only know a few evolutions in the celestial that are human in origin, that are not just heavens with angels with fairy wings floating on clouds. I speak of humans who evolve, make love, have babies, grow, and learn, just as we do here.

There is a world, not one of Castaneda's, where the humans are very tall and graceful. They initially lived here on Earth a million years ago. Many also learned not to die; most eventually walked out as Castaneda did. The DNA remnant of that ancient race of people is still here in a lesser form in the people of the Masai Mara in Africa.

In the world of those ancient people who are now in another dimension, they live in stone houses that seem very organic and pleasing. The houses are small compared to the occupants, so we imagine that they're bigger on the inside than the outside structure might suggest, which in those multidimensional inside-out worlds can be so. Their houses have no doors. They walk through the walls as ingress and egress. It is magical to watch.

Do you see now where grace might take you? It's not just an airy-fairy religious concept that "saved a wretch like me"; it is a real method, an ancient one. It is really most secret and very sacred, and there were people who harnessed the power of it a million years ago, and some of them taught it to us from the Aluna. You have to think wide, very wide, if you seek to arrive. *Try.*

Let's continue. I am not a vital component in anyone's journey, because if you have pure information, you don't need me. And while in the meantime I hope to provide good and accurate instructions as to how to arrive at pure information and the Camelot castle, I wouldn't be the one at the gate who grants access or denies it. That's not my place. I don't have the celestial elevation.

No, I row the boat all day, every day, seven days a week, night and day; and when I find no lords or ladies by the riverside, I sleep a bit. Sometimes an oar breaks and I regrettably have to keep people waiting, and occasionally my other duties take me elsewhere—some of those tasks are very distant, so there's a momentary lull in these activities. But essentially the process is relentless now.

But even when you think there's a lull in your life, much is happening that you can't see, and much is being done to assist you in every way in order that you may arrive. You are loved and watched and assisted, but only as you improve yourself; and if you follow diligently—with dignity, respect, tenderness, and the things that you know are right—the celestial attention of the higher beings descends upon you. I call that "The Gift"—their attention, that is.

Having me for a little while has been helpful to some, but everyone has to take their leave in the end, for if they didn't, they could never become truly individual and free, as the 600 are to be. And I would never go beyond the exigencies of rowing, which I've done for more than two decades.

I love rowing, and seeing people succeed gives me endless pleasure; but, like you, I seek to improve myself. One day I would like to cease rowing people across the river and teaching them the nature of the journey and the ghoul traps to avoid, and I'd like to concentrate on the other tasks that I've now been graciously assigned. For in those new tasks I seek to grow and, hopefully, resonate inside the eternal Tao at a slightly faster level.

Each needs space to grow. Essentially the journey isn't about trying to become someone or something—it is the task of unraveling that which dogma encumbered you with. Learn to become nothing and you will be heading the other way, the correct way. It serves you best never to seek or demand anything much, anything beyond being a part of the Tao. Then you may be given some great role or power; if so, all well and good.

I did seek to row, but only because the task was granted to me. But eventually I would wish to go to the pristine world that I see at my side at 90 degrees. I know I need nothing more. But I'll never ask to go there. I'll wait until it's granted to me, if it ever is.

In my logo are the etheric dogs from the Aluna, hundreds of them, and the Tall Boys—Sacred Beings I've written about before, beings from another evolution that sometimes communicate in silence with hand signals. I can also hear the uilleann pipes from Ireland in my logo and the song of the Shining Ones and much love and merriment; and my wobbly, incoherent dancing is also in there, as well as ". . . laughter, learnt of friends; and gentleness, / In hearts at peace, under an English heaven," as Rupert Brooke wrote in his famous poem "The Soldier." Those words are in there because of my love for them.

In my logo are many other words, many millions of them, and much worn-out leather. I went 3.3 million miles crisscrossing through 60 countries, so "airport" is in my logo. The Lion of Judah is also in there—I have seen so many visions of that being, and I have a great love for him and his lion family. My lily-white back end is also in there, the very same one that I would bend over and point in a very undignified way at the dark forces flying above when outnumbered by them to show them, come what may, I wasn't scared of them anymore. . . . Many things—some beautiful, some not so.

And what can we say of *your* spiritual logo? It will become whatever you decide it should become. If you're cruel and you control, manipulate, rant, and rave, it will become ugly; and you'll be abandoned to your fate. If you go placidly amid the waste, and you selflessly serve those who ask you, your logo will become very beautiful.

You don't need anyone else's help to embrace beauty or to love the Tao, and you don't need anyone to ensure your arrival at the Place of the Orbs. What you need is a warm heart; the Three Graces; and dignity, tenacity, and fortitude—along with the blessing of the eternal Tao, and of course, hard work and humility. For these qualities are seen to be great and good, in an understated way, at the place where the vast eternity of all things was first born—far, far away at that initial place where the eternity that surrounds us today began as just a small, frail spark of golden light seeking to travel, seeking to improve itself and become bigger.

Mount your prayer; pray to the Goddess, for she has all the power, compassion, and healing you will ever need. Ask her to show you a new humility, as from that flows reverence and awe; and then after a few days of asking for these things, ask her to show you the new dignity. If you see it, if she shows it to you, it will dramatically change your life.

⠿ ⠿ ⠿

THE WHITE SHADOW 4

We all have light and dark in our logo that are natural. You can call the logo your soul if you like—maybe that word is easier to understand—but remember that it's not in your chest as a blob of light; it can be the size of a small warehouse, or it could be vast like a galaxy. Yours is very important because it says who you are and surrounds you with a glory or with a darkness, depending. The aspect of the logo that surrounds you drives your karma day to day, dictating what happens to you and how things pan out.

The light side is your passport to another world, a higher perception, more protection, and better worth—more of the healing warmth of grace. Of course, your black shadow is in there along with your good qualities. Almost everyone is aware of evil and what it entails, and some people are prepared to look at the dark inside themselves. I will only mention it in passing here, as I dealt with it at length in my last book, *The Art of Redemption*.

The dark shadow may hide your disdain for the pain of animals and other humans; and it operates in various forms of silent or overt hatred, elitism, snobbery, and isolation. Sometimes it is the predator or the "inner lizard," as I call it, that is competitive, jealous, and mean to people. Extreme forms of the black shadow are violence and cruelty.

It's easy to see it in others, and it's not impossible to see in oneself. But the white shadow is different from the black one—it is very sneaky because you can't usually see the white in yourself and only a few know about it, as people mistake it for goodness and proper living.

The white shadow comes about when you pretend to be holy and good, while deep down you're really evil and have a covert agenda trying to win people over. Or you're seeking to impress them, you're hiding the truth, or you're feeding off them in some way—sexually, say, or financially.

The Mr. Nice Guy pretense, the one that secretly feels better than everyone else, is a white-shadow trait. He hides his assumed superiority and disdain for humanity in social acts of helping and feigned kindness; he plays the white knight. So he greets people at church and raises money for charity; he helps people and makes them laugh; and he often provides for others generously, offering hospitality and entertainment. He is the all-around great guy—and a big phony.

He sees himself as a saint, ignoring his disdain and hatred and his inner violence—which is often expressed against women, and some of it is his indifference toward animals and people. He sees himself as the conquering hero, the man who's always right, while in fact he is cruel and mean and a devil in his soul. This type of man in his white shadow is very common. He is often a liar as well as a womanizer and a fraudster, but he never sees it.

He will often say he loves women, but in fact he hates them silently with a passion, as he seeks to possess

36

them and use them for his gratification. It is the slave-holder's mentality, and sometimes it is vengeance that the man seeks against women, either because he hated his mother or because of sexual frustration. Or at times it is a vengeance he wants to exert at having been rejected by women in the past; or perhaps he is angry because he was ditched by an ex-wife who sued him for money. The white-shadow, white-knight male is often a compulsive liar, as he has to sustain the edifice of his illusions, come what may.

The female version in the white-shadow classification looks like the perfect mother, the wonderful wife, the social organizer, the selfless raiser of children—while she fights with the neighbors and hates other women . . . and she is often a vindictive and racist snob, to boot. She pretends to be the seemingly perfect woman, but under her social niceness, she's cruel and cold. Yet she frivolously imagines she is better than everyone else—whiter, cleaner, more pure. Like the Mr. Nice Guy, she is destined to die in the arms of the ghouls: the phony game player who hides her insidious darkness always finds her true place in hell in the end.

What you do in this life, how often you pay for other people, how many acts of social goodness you perform, or how many children you have raised counts for little. These acts serve only a small part in your redemption; only your deep innermost feelings redeem you. They are what is in your logo—the real you. The way you treat people, criticism, judgments, fighting, and shouting . . . or warmth and a genuine unconditional love—whatever is described in the panorama of the real you, even that which is hidden behind the secret white-shadow thoughts and sentiments, as well as the more overt black ones—*those* are what count.

Here are other common white-shadow examples:

— **Police officers** who pretend to protect society while terrorizing their fellow citizens by taking bribes spray their macho presence over people, controlling them with fear, abusing their power with an ego trip to feel important and worthwhile—the conquering heroes, the protectors, who all the while are inflicting pain as they go.

— **Politicians** who pretend to make life better for people but are only interested in fame and power and care not one iota that the legislation passed controls and milks the citizens, taking them to despair. They act like Moses the Lawgiver, while in effect are like Nazi prison officers: control freaks out to feather their nests.

— **Subversive administrators** are another white-shadow type. Such people get into organizations or committees, and while pretending to be very servile and helpful, they actually undermine the projects as much as they can, backbiting and complaining and using passive aggression to make sure as many things go wrong as can go wrong without anyone actually fingering them. They're immensely covert in the way they seek to bring the house down.

Usually their motivation is jealousy; they are not at the top, so they'll act to make sure those who are have a hard time or look as inefficient as possible. Subversive administrators are in a perpetual silent rage against humanity and often have righteous indignation about the people involved with the tasks at hand or with the organization.

"Important advisors" are often a variation of the administrators' white-shadow traits. Advising is a lot easier than digging the ditch, and one can easily get lost in the importance of the role without ever actually lifting a finger: playing the white-shadow game of the "one in the know," rather than working to achieve a result.

— **Doctors** and **nurses** are often bastions of the same hidden shadow. I knew a nurse once from the Deep South—Texas, I think. She was a virulent racist deep within. I saw that in her and called her on it, and eventually she admitted to me she loved it when African-American people died on her ward and were carted off to the morgue.

That glee in her was hidden behind her white shadow, in which she would do a selfless Florence Nightingale act, pretending to tend to the sick, while hoping they would die, enjoying their pain and the grief of relatives, basking in the power trip of nursing. The would-be living god who has power over life and death is a very enticing place for a corrupt human soul to be. Many nurses and doctors, including surgeons, are very evil.

— **Holy priests** or **monks** can sometimes be in a classically evil white-shadow role in that they see themselves as the representatives of God, but are in effect corrupt and vile, eliminating and downgrading anyone who doesn't believe in whatever silly dogma they do—making people wrong for being different. Those in this category are using a feigned spirituality to hide a darkness, like the thousands of pedophile priests in the Catholic Church who will sit in a booth and listen to people's confessions, without ever looking at *their* crimes against children or humanity.

— We see the same insidious thing in the New Age and alternative-healing business. **Magical healers** who attempt to act as the voice of God, those who are vectoring the energies down for the mere mortals, are deep in the white shadow and often in the disease of the "chosen one": a demonic corruption where humans decide they have been selected to change the world on behalf of God, speaking for God as a preacher might, or vectoring energies—like massage therapists or "hands-on" healers. There they can hide their arrogance behind their supposed service to humanity with a feigned humility.

There is nothing wrong with these kinds of roles—some of them are lovely—as long as you don't fall for the trap of specialness. If you go about your work in relative silence and don't make a performance of it, then it's not the white shadow. The corrupt shaman is one we've seen a lot recently. Many suffer from power lust and a heightened sense of their self-importance, and so many get nobbled (possessed) by the ghouls and go dark, while pretending to be light and white and on the side of Gaia and Mother Earth.

God is the light of grace in all things—it doesn't need people to talk for it. All you have to do is watch a flower bloom, listen to the rain falling, or imagine a scorpion scurrying across pebbles in a desert and you're listening to the words of God. We humans get so high on ourselves, pretending to be specially selected—silly, really.

If you see the white shadow in you—like, say, you do the suffering-servant performance each day—then notice it and unravel it bit by bit and try to become more normal and less fake, less covert. The 11th Commandment ought to be: "Thou shalt not pretend to be normal and nice when in fact you are deeply corrupt and evil." And the 12th might say: "Thou shalt not pretend to serve humanity when in fact you have a covert agenda that seeks importance or intends to milk people instead." We can't have a 13th Commandment—it's an unlucky number.

In the end, the shadow discussion all comes down to this: Will you give up on your ego's obsession, its myopic desire for itself, and your intoxication with the mind and its darkness . . . or will you turn and face the sun, which is an immense source of love? Will you pledge allegiance and loyalty to your sacred journey and the light, or will you side with evil?

If you're genuine, mount your prayer for forgiveness. Look at your white and dark shadows, go into every murky corner of your hidden traits—callousness, say—and pray for clemency, while offering the same to others. If you are genuine, then mouth your prayer every day on your knees and beg God, the higher beings, Gaia, and the trees and the animals and the flowers and the sea and the moon and the stars above . . . beg to be forgiven. Do that prayer on the ground on your knees, head bowed, hands clasped together, for 30 days in a row— more grace will flow and you'll feel lighter. You'll see things.

GRACE, AND HOW PURE INFORMATION FLOWS TO YOU 5

Here is something few people know: grace is vast—we can say with almost certainty that it is omnipresent—but it's still a distinct energy, with complex attributes, just as electricity or microwaves are energies. Microwaves can fry a human body; grace can safely dematerialize it. Grace is lighter than a feather, yet it can lift a human off the ground (levitation).

Grace can show you the Great Void and myriad things, and it also has trillions of components—many of which are beyond our ken—but one thing we do know is that it equates to information. Information and grace are the same. A lack of accurate information is a *dis*-grace. It's caused by your darkness or the cold distance of the mind.

Data-laden grace comes to us in what we call *downloads*. Some are pulses or blips we can feel, and some of them are wide and complicated; usually they come when we're in a meditative state but not always so.

If a download happens, you may feel it as a multi-dimensional impression, like an energy shift in your etheric. You can feel it as sensations: if you're lying on your bed, say, you may feel as if the bed has disappeared and you're hovering in the air; and/or you may have the feeling of turning upside down—your etheric head goes to your feet—or you may feel yourself transported, sliding off at 90 degrees sideways to another world.

There are hundreds of download experiences . . . many people have reported them. Some seem to come at night in dreams. Occasionally you may see the download as little red lines like dashes that are being fired toward you down a funnel that looks like a nonsolid version of a megaphone. The red dashes create a tick-tick sound that you may actually hear, and they build a neon-looking igloo around you that protects you.

Data comes in three forms, a trinity of possibilities:

1. **Normal** (now, 0)

2. **Prophetic** (forward in time in our human future, 1+)

3. **Retrospective** (backward in time, -1)

So we say that it's a binary overlay in its nature, placed either side of zero. So it lies in the relationship between -1 and 0 and 0 and 1+, expressed as: -1 . . . 0 . . . 1+ (backward information, -1; "n0w" information, which we label 0; and information for the future, 1+). That data code, when overlaid, has a multidimensional 90-degree turn in it that's not immediately obvious. If you see it expressed as in a straight line (-1 . . . 0 . . . 1+), you don't usually notice the anomaly in it. But if you see it as two codes (-1 . . . 0 and 0 . . . 1+), then you might see the anomaly. Overlay them and the 90-degree turn becomes obvious.

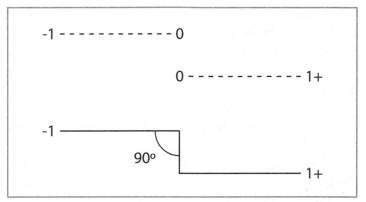

Fig. 3: The 90-degree turn.

So we say that the -1 . . . 0 component is the hazy-wave, nonsolid, quantum state of our humanity; and the 0 . . . 1+ is the solid state.

Simultaneously your physical body exists in a trinity of possible states:

1. **Here** (solid)
2. **Not here**, -1, invisible (not solid)
3. **Over there**, 1+

By "over there," we talk of one of two things: (1) your mirror-self is usually always someplace else, so that's considered normal—that's one form of "over there"; or (2) if you ever go wide enough here in 3-D, then your physical self can be elsewhere as well.

For example, your body is in L.A. at 3:59:58 A.M., and three seconds later it's in New York. The data transfer that describes the total you—arms, head, bones, feelings, and so on—has been deleted in L.A. and uploaded in Manhattan at precisely four o'clock and one second (4:00:01), behind a Dumpster in an alley where you knew no one would see you do it—an alley in New York that you could see in your mind's eye from L.A. before you made the move.

It is very *Matrix*-like, but then again, almost everything from that first *Matrix* film came true. That's why I watched it more than 50 times, because it was the story of what was happening to us at that time. Programs in the "in and out carrier signals" showed us all these amazing things, just as Neo was shown the downloads for kung fu, tae kwon do, and the "jump" program in the film.

Pray every day to see more and learn more. Don't yearn for power; just pray humbly that you might see.

Remember that you don't have to be a saint to have grace flowing into your life. All you need are the Three Graces (*generosity, tenderness,* and *respect*) and things change overnight. Your celestial blindness, and perhaps a lack of information, will be swept away and the doors of perception will open.

As I said, when the Morph descended, I saw at least 100 visions in seven years, probably more . . . I didn't write them all down. There are people I know who are seeing visions at double that rate—great visionaries who are far, far beyond me.

But those early visions were critical. They allowed me and those people I'm charged with helping to understand and harness the healing warmth of grace and arrive at ever more information. What we know now is 10 times more than what we did six months ago, and that's 500 times what we knew before the Morph descended in 2001. Your power to proceed is rapid and endless. This journey is vast—beyond vast.

You came initially from a glorious place, and now you have to remember those things you forgot, those facts that were programmed out of you as a child. Let go, surrender, agree to evolve. If you become more, we *all* become more. Humans are linked. We are all compartments in one global mind, and that global mind is very small—like, say, just one cell in the goddess Kali's finger—but in its diminutive state, it's still valuable to you.

If you're not up in your ivory tower, then everyone has something to teach you. Isolation is a disease of the ego—cold and cerebral. If you embrace humans, you go wider and safer. Rudolf Steiner said that cancer is a cold disease; he was right—jot that down.

There is a link between warmth and openness and the quality of information you receive. We say that information is pure when it comes to you traveling through your humility, balance, and sense of belonging. That information is accurate. What poses as pure information is often inaccurate or bogus.

Here's why: The devilish beings in the Aluna that were formerly humans can talk to your mind just as the celestial can. The ghouls are very crafty about sending people the wrong way, buttering them up to believe some spurious ego trip—we call that a *claridad,* which is Spanish for "clarity." It's a shamans' joke, as claridad is anything but clear: it's when people are led along to believe they're special, like when they come back from a journey with the sacred plants believing that they're Jesus.

When you're offered something in a vision that adds to importance, always decline: the Holy Grail, a special crown, a sword, an exceptional position (the voice-of-God job—tee-hee) . . . whatever you're offered, bow and reject it. Only the gifts that come to you without your knowing about them are genuine; all else is the ghouls towing you by the nose. Beware of importance; anything that offers it is a trap, as is anything that offers a quick fix, a fast buck, or instant elevation—in the real worlds of the celestial, there is no such thing. Drop the idea that you'll suddenly be raised up; that's a fool's paradise—ghoul food.

Then, too, beware of prophetic dreams. People do have them, but it's often just a numbers game. Everyone dreams hundreds of times each night, even if they don't remember doing so. So there are 6.5 billion dreamers on the planet; and, say, this week one hundred million dream of a plane crash, which is often the subconscious mind's way of saying that we're "falling" down with the flu, or it's a symbol of some other collapse of integrity. Then a plane hits the tarmac in Bujumbura, Africa, and they all say, "Wow, I dreamed that."

Other prophetic dreams may be accurate, but they usually come from what you know subliminally. So you dream that the financial deal you're in will fall apart. You went to a meeting today where everyone said "yes-yes," but subliminally you saw the eyes of the big boss go "no-no." These types of dreams are fine, and they're often accurate, but at times they set you back. You may have subliminally seen hesitation in the boss's eyes, but that doesn't mean he or she won't decide in your favor eventually. The prophetic negative dream might wreck your chances if you accept it as fact and sustain that idea for any length of time. See how tricky it can be?

Imagine if you stood outside the supermarket on a busy morning and stopped people to ask what they thought you ought to do about the sex problems you're having with a boy- or girlfriend. All those who had time to discuss it would gladly do so, as humans like giving advice, and after a little while you'd have 30 versions of what you might need to do to solve the matter of the nauseating traits of your insignificant other—latest squeeze—whatshisbloodyname?

Spirits are no different: they need to be *needed*. You may very well be channeling the Pleiadians, but the question arises whether they know dilly-squat from Shinola or not.

For example, there is a band of energy close to Earth that looks like a ring of Saturn, made up of what I call the "flashy-faces." You often see them in your mind's eye just as you start to meditate, as you move out of 3-D toward a more multidimensional consciousness. Some of those faces are of dead people, and some are still alive on Earth; some are angry, some benign; some look scary, some normal. If you hesitate in the band, you'll start to hear five-word snippets—short sentences that sometimes seem to be missing a bit at the end and sometimes not—I named them yum-yums: "The horses look so very . . ." "He didn't make the cake," "Why are the flowers dead?" and so on.

Sometimes the yum-yums are accurate. I heard one that said, "The ships take three days." Then I read in the paper that morning of some warships that would take three days to arrive in the Gulf.

Most of the snippets are gibberish. They are audio feeds from the collective unconscious mind, bits of other people's mental conversations or thoughts blipping into your mind. If you take those yum-yums as Gospel truth, rack and ruin will soon follow. Just as the people at the supermarket might be very well-meaning, but may know absolutely nothing about your sex life.

Interestingly, when you hear the yum-yums, you will feel that your etheric has gone upside down and left to right . . . as if it has shifted north to south, say, and twisted from west to east—and vice versa. This is because the subconscious mind is upside down and left to right in its relationship with the outside 3-D world. That's how the brain is designed. So when you're in the flashy-faces band, you feel that pole shift take place etherically, as that's a facet of the dimension you're watching.

If people are very dark or even slightly dark, their shadows are like floaties swirling in the bowl, unprocessed, "unflushed." Then the ghouls will be around them, close to their skin or even inside their bodies. They create intestinal indigestion and an irritable bowel . . . these are ghoul-related problems, and a lack of accurate spiritual information stems from that ghoul proximity. It's a corruption that flows to the mind while showing that the humans stand in a lack of grace because their darkness has called in the ghouls and housed them on a long-term basis. This may be because the individuals' bad karma is still hanging close, and so the ghouls latch on in response to that.

I've always felt that a large percentage of humans are abducted by the ghouls without ever knowing it. Later, via the Aluna, I discovered this to be a fact. The bewitchment of humans can be mild, but I've also dealt with versions of it that are extreme in the form of full demonic possession. The power of the ghouls to infiltrate is very great. I worked as an exorcist for a while—it's a rotten job, and the pay is terrible. Try to avoid that line of work if you can.

Pure information flows when you're pristine, calm, and serene. When you're disturbed or deep in your darkness, information flow may quicken, but it will be the *wrong* information, and you'll soon be wasting thousands visiting moldy monks in Tibet. Never go to Tibet, avoid Jamaica (the pot calls in the ghouls), and don't go to Israel—unless you're Jewish; then it's okay.

There is a dimension peopled by beings I call the *Nutters,* a name derived from English slang: *nutcase*— "nutter"—a demented or unstable person. They are humans who are still alive, floating about elsewhere in the world in their spirit form—their mirror-self identity—doing strange things.

The Nutters are common. You see them in fancy hotels a lot, as there's an elitism there that workers react to negatively. I saw one guy in his spirit form in a waiter's outfit with a tray of drinks standing in a fountain, as well as the spirit of a maid spooning mayonnaise into the pockets of jackets hanging in guests' closets. These are real humans alive today, but they appear as spirit beings: it is the Aluna-self of humans who are asleep or even people who are awake someplace in the world, in an alter ego—we can see them quite clearly. One of the Nutters was standing next to a friend of mine in a hotel restaurant in a waitress's outfit, swinging a cat over her head.

They are so bizarre and funny to watch, but there is something spooky about them, as they seem so demented. It's the stress of modern living that flips these people and sends them slightly around the bend. So the maid's desire for vengeance, her jealousy, makes her Aluna-self spoon mayo into people's clothing because her real 3-D self doesn't have the courage to do so (for fear of losing her job, perhaps). There are billions of spirits right here, right now that one can't normally see, and they can talk—eek! If the Nutters are speaking—advising you about your sex life, say—they're bound to send you the wrong way just out of spite.

Ham slices is the term I give to telepathic interferences coming into your mind, thoughts that you may realize aren't your own. Sometimes they're embarrassingly derogatory of someone you're with whom you might love and care for enormously. Maybe you've had this experience. It's as if someone has sliced into your mind with a ham-slicing machine, like at the deli. Sometimes the ham slices are derogatory of you and try to bring you down by indicating your failings, making much of your minor shortcomings, or playing to a deep insecurity. These ham slices are ghouls talking, and they're almost always to your right, coming in from about head height. When you feel them coming in to interrupt your natural train of thought, turn your head to the right, blow love on them, and say "Begone."

Karma and pure information are linked. Some people are born with rotten karma. They've had lives as ugly people in the past, and they're here to hopefully ameliorate that karma without complaining too much. The advanced soul suffers in silence—remember that.

Most karma is instant stuff that you accumulated in this life. For example, if you're into pornography—obsessed by it, say—that is the slaver's mind-set, one that seeks to make an unknown stranger into a submissive sex partner. That mentality calls to the ghoulishness that is in the spirits of dead humans who were formerly rapists or men and women who hurt others for sexual pleasure. Or, it calls in dead homosexual boys who used to bonk strangers in toilets—shadow traits—the ghouls ride them like hobos ride the trains at night across lonely and bleak lands.

People don't realize how pornography might give them cancer. There is a certain type of ghoul, a wizened creature about the size of a garden-gnome statue—it is very ugly and gnarly; its speciality is cancer, and it promotes the disease. Cancer cells are radicals that feed off the body to its detriment, without its knowledge, just as the porno man might feed off the bodies of others without *their* knowing, to *their* detriment—same ilk. Innocent cancer victims? Not always, no.

So when the porno king or queen requests advice and inspiration in prayer or meditation, a torturer from the 1700s may answer, and that ghoul torturer in the Aluna may abuse the person who's praying and asking for help and tow him or her around by the nose as that human, in turn, abuses and restricts others.

The celestial has no time for impurities. By that I don't just mean that personal hygiene (which, of course, is important) is lacking, but also a lack of integrity, a lack of warmth—dishonesty, usury, sexual perversions, feeding off people, or a disrespect for the divine and/or animals and humans—or a lack of the Three Graces.

Pure information doesn't care to visit the corrupt. It doesn't come to rescue people from their degradations. It is sent through the 3-D Matrix from a place that is pristine, full of reverence, honor, care, and love. The radiant hues of that information flow in quanta that are bathed in a celestial light of great worth and clarity. It is a manufactured ray of light delicately poised in a fine symmetry, like the beams of a rainbow that are carefully spaced, with all the colors of the spectrum present . . . a beam of information that is graciously directed toward you—when and if it comes. You must always wait patiently.

If the intended recipient isn't of the same purity, if the person isn't as translucent as the beam, then the pulse of light of that download of information isn't sent, or it gets caught by the ghouls that are attached to the grubby human and is infected by a nuance of malicious intent and flipped over.

This happens regularly. The information feels real to the human—special, even—but it's tumbled, and "do this" becomes "don't do this" in less than a split second. It is an adverse knock effected by the ghouls, a contradiction, a distortion of trajectory like those Japanese pachinko machines where the little ball tumbles at random from the top of the machine, hitting pins as it goes, falling left and right to land randomly in a hole at the bottom; the more ghouls around you, the more pachinko distortions.

The celestial is drawn to simplicity, purity, beauty, and a reverence that is natural, which comes from deep within your silent power. Try gradually to nurture those things in your heart, and pure downloads will come to you from the Aluna, flowing into your conscious mind little by little over the days and weeks to come. They become your teacher, and they set you free of dogma to grow ever more natural and pristine. They come in sleep, but mostly they come when you're sitting in silence—on a park bench, for instance. The downloads can give you information that no human has ever been taught before. We have had hundreds of those unique items of information. Things no one knows.

The karma of misinformation has much to do with the ghouls cluttering the netlike Matrix. Initially we thought that the ghouls built the Matrix as a control trip over humans. We weren't sure, but we thought this was so because it was suggested in the film of the same name.

But, eventually, as we grew in complexity and understanding, we came to see that the Matrix, while it *is* a net over us, is one that comes out of (emerges from) the fractal codes of 3-D, and its construct is what holds 3-D from bursting apart in a big bang. We see the Matrix as a dome-shaped hexagonal mesh, as pictured here. I've seen it maybe 400 times, and others see it all the time as well, so we know that it's there.

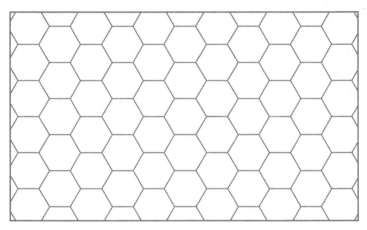

Fig. 4: The hexagonal Matrix.

I think that in very ancient times, the Matrix used to be a pure crystalline net. It's just that over time the ghouls landed in its mesh to control and corrupt it, so each one acts like a black blob interfering with information coming through from beyond the Matrix, from the celestial worlds—it's as if the ghouls are hanging from the netting.

And for a long time—eons—no one was allowed out of the Matrix. There was no way out. The ghouls made sure of that. It was our collective karma to stay inside it and not see very much. We were required to study and be absorbed and trapped in the clutch of the mundane and to suffer the interference/evil of the ghouls, which humans have had little precise information about. The Morph lit it all up for us, so that's how we now know. That's how we learned to fight to change it.

If you care about the flow of clean information, you need purity—purity of thought and emotions, serenity and calm, no self-pollution, silent walks, fasting, quiet time, decent organic food, little fat, no junk. I don't insist that people become vegetarians, but I can say to you that no person who has ever made it to the Lake of Avalon was a meat eater. You need Gaia—without her you have no chance, and eating her children scores zip. It turns you into a foul spirit, so *you* decide.

It isn't hard to understand why purity and information are linked; but, in contrast, the ghouls are dirty, unclean spirits, so that tells you. It's all about a purity of being that emerges gradually from your respect and tenderness. So many people hate the divine, and they degrade it with their words and feelings, mocking it. It is most foolish.

Become the protector of soft sentiments, not their destroyer. Start with love—make yours a pure love, one that's rarely seen. No agenda, no expectations, no covert games, no eking it out a little here and a little there. Love everything and everyone; and those you *can't* love because they're so evil, then at least respect them and be neutral toward them. Have no ill will or rancor, criticisms, or judgments; and don't play the phony victim—stay inside the protection of the Tao.

Acceptance is the key: agree with the way the world and its people are, and become the protector of grace and the feminine spirit. If you seek to escape, free yourself of encumbrances and silly ideas. We need you to make a run for it—come now if you can; it's quite urgent . . . there is little time left.

TRANSDIMENSIONAL DOWNLOADS TO HELP YOU 6

Remember *Aluna* is a Spanish word that describes what we call the mirror-world, which is a vast dimension that is facing us where things appear left to right, as if in a mirror . . . the place where your spiritual double exists—the mirror-self.

Stretch your arm out in front of you, and about halfway down your forearm, between your elbow and your wrist, you enter physically into the Aluna—it's that close. So in that outstretched position, your lower forearm, wrist, and fingers are in another world. If the Morph is strong and the light is dim, they will dematerialize and disappear. This has been reported by thousands of people so many times that it's not in doubt anymore.

Sentient Beings

The idea of sentient beings from another world may make you queasy with disbelief and apprehension. I understand. Astronomy tells us that there are billions of galaxies; and each may have a hundred billion or more stars, many of which have planets . . . so trillions

59

of planets are possible. The idea that there may be life like us on one or more of those trillions of planets isn't so crazy. But even if a technologically advanced society exists far away, there is no way of transferring data from there to here in less than many light-years, so intergalactic information is unlikely.

When we realized that information we didn't previously know was being transferred to us, we imagined correctly that it must come from inner space, not outer space—we know that there's no real distance in inner space. Those inner-space worlds are constructed from light, and photons don't follow the Pauli exclusion principle, which requires solid particles to occupy separate places in the universe. So a solid planet and its solid beings would also have to follow the Pauli principle, which creates immeasurable distances across which information from solid sources might have to travel through the vastness of the Universe. Photons can occupy the same space, overlaid on each other, just as the binary zeros mentioned before are overlaid, so numerous dimensions can technically be placed on a pinhead.

Let me digress for a moment. A programmer who knows a special language wrote letters and codes that instruct a distant computer—on another continent, maybe—to download a complex video and audio track to your screen. Almost instantly you're watching and listening to a song on YouTube. You don't pray for the soul of that programmer who brought you the free song to entertain you; you don't see the person as a highly evolved, sacred being; and more often than not, you don't even think about the miracle of the complexities he or she knows and willingly shares. You just click and listen.

The Aluna downloads are much the same. There are sentient beings at the other end of them that you know nothing about, highly technological beings. The downloads that are sent to you are manufactured packages of data, and they flow along an information highway that we see as long colored tubes, just as a song is sent down the Internet.

Now working back as a proof, albeit a nonabsolute, this is how we came to the conclusion that sentient beings from other dimensions are downloading information to us:

The first piece of good evidence came as a video I watched with one other person present that played spontaneously on the wall of a friend's living room for 45 minutes without any human-made device to create the images. It was a film of a cat fighting with dark beings in a forest. I wrote about that high-strangeness in my previous book.

Several other black-and-white videos followed that played on the walls unexpectedly. One was a short film, a few minutes long, of dinosaurs grazing with their offspring on grasslands; and there followed a short clip of animals today on what I thought might be the Serengeti, also grazing.

Next, visions followed, thousands of them—accurate ones—but the best proof came from the four-color videos that play in the mind's eye. Now one could say that it's all a hallucination, the stupidities of deranged people, and that well could have been true. But if a four-color video plays for two hours, and part of the information tells you to tell a friend that his mother in Kenya is sick, and if he does indeed have a mother in Kenya, a fact you didn't know, and she is unwell . . . then the reality of these downloads becomes ever more certain.

And that is how we came to believe over time: thousands of verifiable bits of information from hundreds of hours of videos that played in the mind's eye and maybe 300,000 to 400,000 visions spread over 15 to 20 different people I know personally to corroborate and back up what I have seen (they often added to it)—pure information that eventually couldn't be contradicted.

Sometimes the beings communicating would refer to a conversation I had with someone in Starbucks the day before, or they would tell me about a meeting that was to happen the next day. So they might say, when Mr. So-and-So arrives at the airport from America, he will say A and B; please respond with X, Y, and Z. And sure enough, the man *did* arrive and he *did* say exactly what the beings said he would say.

Eventually, in our minds' eyes we even began to see the sentient beings that we were communicating with, so that was very exciting. They appear as images on film, like a TV news anchor, except one feels one is in the room that they're broadcasting from. They speak from a gunmetal-gray pod that looks a bit like a papaya, except it's much bigger: it's the size of two blocks of high-rise apartments bolted together. The pod has spikes on it, so it's well protected from the ghouls. It's placed close to us in inner space—it's not an outer-space, alien-beings, UFO thing.

The beings that hack the input/output carrier signals of the Matrix travel down a vortex from some high place to arrive at the pod to make the broadcasts. They're not in there day to day, minute by minute, as it is too close to Earth for their long-term comfort and safety. The broadcasts can last a few seconds or even two hours, and they usually come through about three times a week.

Then there were some beings that we've never seen. They only communicated via audio—not the audio-video pod system—which is still very real and impacting, of course, but different. There is one I love very dearly . . . I named her Mofie. That's because she has a very matter-of-fact way of speaking with an unhurried calm even when there's great danger. Mofie's name comes from an acronym of matter-of-fact voice (MOFV). She is one of the watchers. She protects us. She attends day and night while her human charges are awake. She comments on passing danger in the street; or sometimes she even communicates very mundane things, like one night walking through an ally, she said, "Mind the dog poo," just as the next step was destined for it. But very important information comes from her as well.

Beyond the immediate mirror-world dimensions opposite us that we know about are many more. How we describe them is by first saying where they are. So when facing north, there is a dimension in front of us up at 45 degrees and to the right. So if you point to NNE, halfway between north and east, raising your arm up at 45 degrees above you, that's where the dimension of 45-up, right, is. It is very holy and spiritual—it is where the Sacred Beings and helpers seem to come from—and of course, there may be many different dimensions in that direction.

In the direction that's directly in front of you (north, we call it) and up at 45 degrees is a dimension that looks like the magical forests as seen in fairy books, with unicorns that neigh and the beings we describe as *fawns:* half-deer and half-human. Mofie is a fawn—half-female, half-deer—strange but true.

I used to use the term *hybrid* to describe these half-and-half evolutions, but I never liked the word, as it sounds like a Frankenstein food—like a genetically modified tomato—so I called those Sacred Beings *manimals:* half-man, half-animal. Of course, many are female, so they ought to be womanimals, but that is a bit too much of a tongue twister, so I have rested with "manimals" to describe both the male and female ones.

It is hard to write about the manimals, as it seems so very unlikely and rather dippy. But the mythological figures such as the Minotaur are real in the Aluna, and that's why people knew of them thousands of years ago. They are very high up on the scale of goodness and power in the song-breath of Gaia. They became very important to us and our understanding of things.

They seem to be, in essence, custodians of the Renewal, which we understand as the act of giving the planet back to the animals and creating what I term the *Brave New World,* to borrow Huxley's title: a world that is eventually ghoul free, where no more negative influences remain, so there's no more serious sickness (or very little), few premature deaths, no mental troubles, and no more strife among humans . . . essentially a heaven on earth.

There are other beings that look human to us, except they're 60 feet tall and radiant like gods. They shimmer in gold and iridescent hues of immense beauty, a rainbow's light twists and turns in slow motion through them, and there flows out from their being digital-fractal lines of information akin to vast filigree lace that spread like the branches of a vine . . . sweeping appendages of purple and blue that look like chiffon stretching out for hundreds of yards on either side. It's staggering in its beauty. It took me weeks to get over the sight of it, and the being I saw only showed me a part of her left shoulder and her left arm. I never really saw the entirety.

In the end, our various relationships to these god-like beings became very significant, as we found that we had functions to perform. Some of the Aluna worlds are those of love and bliss; and then there are, as I've said, also hell worlds in there, ones that we were eventually taught to see.

The beings showed us how to fight, sometimes moving our hands very fast in hand-to-hand fighting, sometimes firing darts off our fingers that were given to us, sometimes in other ways. If you learn to move your hands fast, it serves you, as the ghouls are scared of it. In the past I could move mine so quickly that the ghouls would first go eggshell blue, then dematerialize completely. But I'm older and slower now, although I can still do it as a party trick if I really have to, which is very rarely. I only do it nowadays to make the kids laugh.

Now, this next bit will probably sound nuts to you, but it's true, I swear. The beings gave us armor that they built and attached on us little by little over a number of years—etheric armor that was constructed by data-signals coming from beyond the Matrix. Now that really *was* a saving grace! Until we got that, we couldn't operate well, if at all.

Humans, dark ones, prickle like stinging nettles. It's really nasty. The barb of their hatred forms sharp needles that travel across the intervening space to strike you etherically, and you feel it as real pain on your skin. It's excruciating, and the stinging effect can jump right across a freeway from drivers going in the other direction, so a simple road trip becomes agonizing hell.

The stinging-nettle sensation seems quite random, striking all over your body. Sometimes the hits leave small red triangular marks on your skin. They can come every few seconds, so you can't really take your mind off them, and if the nettles hit you in the private parts, they can drop you to the floor in pain. The intensity of humans' ability to sting is calibrated to their level of evil.

Initially the armor we got was a bit rudimentary—it stopped most of the nettles but by no means all of them. But eventually the beings got really sophisticated and/or our energy and comprehension rose, and the anti-nettle armor became close to invincible.

Once outfitted, we found that we could go into the Aluna to abolish the ghouls in their hell worlds in great numbers. They're so disgusting and depraved that they make you feel dirty—you think there is no soap or scrubbing brush that can remove their imprint from your skin. We got good at it—fighting, that is, not the washing part.

One night I was on my bed and had my hands in the air in the Aluna, and I could see the ghouls lit up in a mystical blue-gray light. On them appeared hundreds of cactus spines. They looked so mysterious that I didn't know what to make of them. "What do I do with these?" I asked. I heard: "Point." In the distance I could faintly see a ghoul's face, so I pointed and it melted and died.

Gradually my sight of the ghouls and the worlds they exist in became ever more sensitive and accurate. I found that I could enter their worlds within six seconds after closing my eyes. Gradually I got the courage to travel ever deeper into ones so horrific that they defy description: worlds of grotesquely deformed humans, monsters with three heads, and hundreds of different types of evil—all crooked and bent out of shape, all angry, and all attacking as I approached.

I learned to be fast on my feet. The ghouls spit and fire pulses at you. One of our human fighters rubbed out 135,000 ghouls in just a couple of weeks. I've terminated about 70,000 so far, at a rate of about 300 a day. I pray that they evolve to something better, but fighting the ghouls is all too dangerous to be hanging about, worrying about their evolution. Their deaths bring us more light. You have to think of the ghouls as black imps, blobs of evil hanging off the Matrix net: the more that are knocked off, the easier it becomes for information to flow unimpeded.

Then there are hosts of other good spiritual beings in the inner worlds that perform every manner of function. I'm reluctant to speak of those beings and their functions for fear of being considered ever more dippy. But we know of many evolutions that are so incredibly beautiful that they defy definition; watching them evokes bliss. And some of the beings are so powerful that we can't comprehend them. I've written about one goddess we know of in the chapter called "The Goddess of a Trillion Universes."

These beings are communicating now in order to help humans evolve quickly enough to manage, for these are the End of Days before the Renewal; and lest you think this is limited to some clique around me, I assure you that such is not so. There are thousands of humans I've never met who know about the downloads—some have e-mailed me on the subject, so that's how I surmise that many people around the world have had the downloads that allow them to peer into other worlds, people who know about the Sacred Beings.

Now here is something very strange that many of us have seen: There are humans alive today who are so high up that they're in a "manimal" as well as a human form. That is, there are those who exist in more than one incarnation at once. They are spiritually very wide. You have to imagine a human with Aluna-deer's horns on his head or whose head or body is partly that of an eagle with feathers. There are others who are brown with fur: ones who belong to the bear tribes.

It was taught to us that these humans alive today who have manimal incarnations arrive at that elevation because they have such a strong connection to the Tao— they evolve to become the magical beings that exist in other dimensions. So their part-human, part-animal life is concurrent with their regular human evolution. Remember that the animal evolutions are closer to the Tao, so they're higher than we are. Humans aren't at the top of the scale by a long chalk. The manimal incarnations are eternal but on a different loop.

Let's go back to the information about reincarnation for a moment. We talked about the Golden Radiant Being that you eventually became, and so as not to confuse you, I put that being on the same Möbius strip as your human incarnations. In fact, the being is at the place we call 45-up, right, on another loop that's connected.

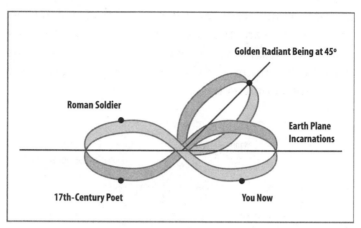

Golden Radiant Being Dimension at 45° from Earth Plane

Fig. 5: The extension of the Möbius strip.

So it's placed on what looks like a petal of a flower still linked eternally to your human lives but at a 45-degree tangent. Now if you draw a line at 90 degrees to the level plane of the Möbius strip, that's where the manimals and some more of the celestial worlds are. It's another petal.

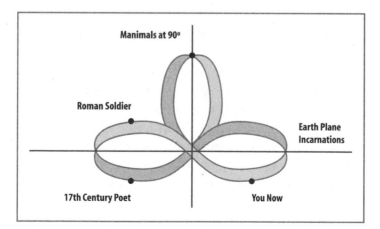

Fig. 6: The manimal loop.

How many there are in total isn't known by me. The wider you are, the more you're connected to many existences. The more existences you have concurrently with this life, the more information flows to you and the more protection you have.

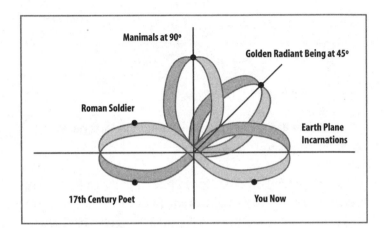

Fig. 7: The 3-D loop with two hyper-dimensional loops.

Trip Codes

Some of the Aluna information that comes to you isn't transmitted directly from the beings; it operates on a system of trip codes. Some codes are in words that you read; some are in music. So, for example, a series of notes in a song can take your soul off to the 90-degree world, and once there, you'll learn information of current value to you. Sometimes the trip codes evoke an ancient memory of who you used to be, where you once belonged— messages from your spiritual home, let's say, calling back to you, reminding you to be strong and not to give up.

Some codes are timeline codes—*positioning effects*, we say. The picture or information of the "future you" is encrypted in a digital-fractal quanta of information that's placed out ahead of you in time so that you may arrive. It's like a visualization where you see yourself at some pleasant future state, except it's more complicated than that.

The "positioning effect" is an artifact from the Aluna that allows you to arrive at your proper destiny. Imagine it as a block of information placed five years out ahead of you to assist you in achieving a spiritual progress. In essence, it's an insertion into your logo that describes *where* you will arrive in the end, not so much *how* you will get there. It's the way the destiny of the world arrives eventually at its pristine state—one of love, not one of hate.

Some of the trip codes are set in items/artifacts that are triangular in shape. These items have been deliberately manufactured by good beings and placed on Earth from the Aluna to help people. The triangles are blue-gray in color; they're usually set on a post, gate, or doorway, down low for the children. They look a bit like the swing door of a Western saloon, except they're triangular, not oblong, and you can see through them. They're about two feet long from base to apex.

So imagine a triangle sticking out from a door frame that people walk through without knowing it's there. The triangle is cleverly placed on wide doors so that some individuals will trip it and many won't—it only partly covers the gap. Contained in the speckled ambience of the triangle is potential information for that person. Some Aluna artifacts are not triangular but brick shaped.

Then there must be many codes I know little about, like in the songs of birds. The birds deliver fractal codes of great beauty. We can actually see these as colorful geometries that leave their throats. Each chirp means something to the overall prayer that's calling you back to the heartbeat of Gaia. Their voices are part of the beauty of it all, a part of the secret war.

All animals have trip codes in their sounds. Listen to the songs of whales, for example; you know that it means something when you hear it.

The ghouls got in the Matrix and corrupted it, sending humans the wrong way. That's why I say it's all written backward—the hell worlds are cold, not hot. If you look for the opposite, you'll almost always be right. So misinformation is one of the vital functions of ghouls—remember that they can talk to your mind and make it sound as if it's your voice that you're listening to.

The ghouls are very dark and deformed and full of anger and hate; and they align you to sickness, disease, and despair. As I said, they trap you via importance. Their power trip seeks to own you and control you, as that feeds their importance.

Aluna downloads from them are everywhere, and they're stored in humans, as well as artifacts that float through the air. They corrupt pure information. Watch them all the time.

A human's evil downloads to others—it's often placed in etheric balls a little bigger than golf balls. They seem to be heat-seeking for body warmth. The balls come off the dark person at shoulder height, float across a room, and dive into your crown chakra, infesting your higher knowing.

I've seen those etheric balls enter humans' heads hundreds of times. It is fascinating but sad to watch, as I know that the person will be worse for it. How you protect yourself from this infiltration is by grace and purity. Your safety is based on the integrity of your journey.

So, for example, if you walk past a sex-addict porno man in the street, there is darkness there, as the ghouls will own him because of his slaveholder mentality and his yellow-pus etheric. Sometimes a line of information that looks like a tube of black liquid will secretly be projected by him and his ghoul controllers out to passersby. It's an induction process. And so you might suddenly feel horny and imagine yourself in a violent sexual fantasy or some perverse domination scenario. You are sucked into the porno king's world—momentarily abducted.

Or, a person's silent hate will flip to you, and you'll call your spouse and provoke a fight. The ghouls promote conflict and arguments as a way of taking people away from Zen, serenity, and order . . . to disorder and chaos.

Just as the Aluna triangles hang at some doors to rescue you, the ghouls manufacture large etheric structures that they use to take people the other way. Often these are large fractal cubes that hover over a city square, for instance, several hundred feet up. They act as surveillance devices, part of the system of watchers, and they fire detrimental codes into people walking about. Some are very large: about the size of the dome of the Capitol in Washington, D.C., say. The first of these stations that I saw was over a town called Puebla in Mexico, but they are everywhere.

The ghouls have many devices, and the drone-beings that they create and manufacture, such as the Greys, promote the Empire of Snake, as I call it.

For example, the Men in Black that are part of the UFO mythology are real. They are an example of drone-beings that promote evil. They're not real; they're manufactured/created entities.

They first appeared in the late '40s as the UFO mystery began. When people first saw them, they always appeared in zoot suits and kipper ties, and they were sometimes seen driving a version of an American car of that era with the fins at the back. The Men in Black seem to have a stuck-in-time quality that many people have reported. They have been upgraded in recent years, and the modern Men in Black wear single-breasted suits, more Prada looking.

They come usually in groups of nine. They stand in a row in a city square and infect pedestrians by touching them etherically. They promote disease and misery, acting as one collective drone-mind, just as the Greys do. If you kill a Man in Black, it drops to the floor as a pile of gray ash, and then the other eight in the line experience great fear and also drop to oblivion, but it takes about 30 minutes for the process of degrading them to take place. They're seen in forests as well, but we don't know what they do there.

Of course, alcohol and drugs disrupt the celestial carrier signals of the downloads, as they diffuse your mind, making it go out of focus and hazy. In the Matrix, the power of the ghouls is sometimes seen as an amorphous, hazy blob. Whatever you're looking at that's behind the blob becomes unclear and hard to see, like images in a diffused lens. So addictions have to be watched.

The sacred plants such as Ayahuasca and psilocybin mushrooms are good when approached in a reverent way. They open channels in the Aluna that go very deep. However, depending on your approach, they will take you to both the dark worlds and the light.

Gradually, as the ghouls die as a result of the current Aluna wars between good and evil, the carrier signals to decent humans will improve in clarity.

Aluna Pop-ups

Some information comes to you in a very strange way. Let me explain. I often wondered if it was possible to download information directly onto one's computer from the digital-fractal worlds in the Aluna. They operate on the same binary, digital, on-off system that our computers do; and ours are very funky compared to the inner-world systems of the beings, which we know are very high tech.

For example, if you have a five-megapixel camera, your photos will have five million pixels. The word *pixel* is, as you may know, short for "picture element," so five million dots of resolution. In the Aluna, there is a world that we know of that is 50 times higher in resolution than the most advanced photography in the world, so 250 million pixels.

The clarity is beyond comprehension. It's stunning. It really impacts one to see it and to know that such a technology exists. Imagine a dimension that's 50 times more detailed in color and preciseness per square inch than our world and its most modern technology.

While I was working on the Diana, Princess of Wales, conspiracy thing some years ago—writing about it, going to Paris, seeing visions about it—I hoped that I could get a digital download from the Aluna of an audio or audio-video of a crucial meeting that took place in a palace in England where a number of important people were present. That meeting was when I believe, rightly or wrongly, that the Diana "hit" was planned.

At the time, my wish was probably pie-in-the-sky, hoping for the evidence to download from another dimension, but I'd leave my computer on at night with messages indicating my hoped-for desire regarding the critical missing evidence. Eventually beings came in to tell me that the Diana story wasn't my gig, that it would eventually come out and cause great consternation among the British people, but that the outing of it was going to be handled in another way—by others, I presume.

But it was during the time when I was hoping for the evidence to download that I had my first Aluna pop-up. An Aluna pop-up occurs when, say, you're in Microsoft Word, your Internet browser is on in the background, and a Google page comes up without your entering any information in the search engine or even clicking on the site. So you might be thinking about something and the correct page containing helpful information suddenly appears as if from nowhere—sometimes it even happens when you step away to get a coffee. I'm not talking about pop-up ads for Viagra or holidays in Hawaii . . . I'm saying that a coherent Google page pops up about something one is thinking about or working on.

One of the Aluna experts I know, a friend named Udita Chohan, told me that she had 15 Google pop-ups in two months. One pop-up from the Aluna was a photo of a really cute white lion that suddenly appeared one day on her computer screen when she was feeling a bit low. My friend loves animals. On another occasion, she was thinking about hummingbirds, as she'd seen a vision of them at a sacred lake, and suddenly a song started to play via her iTunes software. It was a track of Celtic music, and the video that went with it featured hummingbirds hovering over a lake.

One day a picture of an ancient castle popped up, and she didn't know what to make of it, but she saved it and later told me about it. A week after that, the Sacred Aluna

Beings came in and said that my son had had an incarnation at that castle in some past age and that I should take him there in the summer. It's all so mysterious.

Skype, as you may know, is a system for making phone calls and sending chat messages with a computer. You register your Skype name of choice before going on the system for the very first time. My friend Udita used the initials of her first name and her married name as her Skype name. Then one night when her computer was completely shut down, with no power to it, the beings went and changed her Skype name from her initials to her spiritual name and added the number 26. We believe that the world of the beings is 26-dimensional, as suggested by Michio Kaku in his book *Hyperspace.*

So her Skype name went from her initials to the new name without her knowing how the switch was made. She was astounded, as she has little computer knowledge and wouldn't have any idea how to change her Skype name if she wanted to.

I calculated that it took a total of 11 mouse clicks or keystrokes to make her Skype name change. It's a mystery how the beings know what selections to make in the drop-down menu and how they know to choose them in the right order to make the required change.

It's beyond extraordinary how pure information can communicate now. But we now know that the transfer of digital data directly to a computer is possible from the Aluna, as some force must be entering it in the computer without any human pressing the keys or clicking the mouse here in 3-D.

If these otherworld pop-ups and computer actions are indicative of the power of the inner beings, then maybe the hard evidence of crimes will appear one day, or information that's not retrievable elsewhere might be given. I may never get the Diana evidence from the Aluna worlds—I know that—but other things may come.

Strangely, as I was writing this, a YouTube video popped up. I didn't even have that Website open at the time, and it began playing spontaneously of its own accord. It was of an Italian journalist talking about the fourth secret of Fatima and a secret society in the Vatican called Servizio Informazioni del Vaticano, which is like the CIA branch of the Catholic Church.

Interesting? I'm not sure right now what that information has to do with me, but maybe I'll find out later. The collapse of the Pope and the Roman Catholic Church is due later, so it may be connected to that.

It's all real. These tales are real; the man who walked through the wall is real; the Lake of Avalon is a real place; the Shimmering Door, the portal to the Camelot world that I write about, is a real thing; the Renewal is real; and the beings are real, more so than we are, as they're higher than we are. All that you need to arrive is grace, and that comes in part from dignity and an absence of malice, which is vital for you. Trust me—I've carried so many people. Trust and follow these simple methods I lay out here.

Additional note: I have a friend named Khris Krepcik—he's from Nebraska—whom I consider to be one of the world's experts on the input/output carrier signals, the fractal cube, and the downloads. I go to him for advice on these subjects all the time. I asked him to do a short piece on the topic, which I've included in the Appendix. I think you'll find it interesting; he has called it "The Matrix and the Human Soul."

THE END OF DAYS

Human beings are very important to the Aluna world and the overall spiritual process. We are a major species, and even the radiant beings of the hierarchies are human looking, so they must have been alive as humans before, even if they weren't on Earth but someplace else.

But, as I said, humans are very evil, and we live in a secret dimension of darkness all around us. There are a number of us who can see the innermost feelings of people in the street by watching the fractal codes that surround them. It's more than looking at their aura; it's much more detailed. We can see their incarnations and the overall record of their life—major events, say. I give you my word that there are only one or two normal people out of every hundred who pass by. A few others (four, say) are warm but troubled; and the rest are cold, living devils wandering in our midst. Many are intensely egocentric and evil, yet they wander about pretending to be normal.

These devilish humans incubate ghouls at home in pods that they know nothing about, ones that hang from the ceiling and eventually break open to spawn more evil in the district. Or the humans carry the ghouls around with them in their bellies or chests, and they also deliver the etheric golf balls I spoke of.

We can watch it, so we know. They are part of the control mechanism of the dark forces. There are billions of them . . . some are your lovers. Eek! As the human population rose to more than six billion, the dark power of the Empire of the Snake grew exponentially. There was more heat and more people the ghouls could use— that's why I say we live in an evolution that is descending, not ascending, as we think it is. When there were fewer people on Earth, our spirituality was more organic, indigenous, and natural.

The ghouls gradually infested the trees, forests, and crops; and they bothered the animals, making them sick. They eventually crept into every corner of the world except places that are very remote. They secretly captured our human evolution and our progress, even though most humans have no idea of it or they would fiercely deny it. It is the power of the modern technological Matrix to dominate ideas and humanity and to blind us and send us in the wrong direction. Humanity became lost, and nature started to die. So the gods reincarnated as humans in this current age to put an end to it all.

The Morph takes oxygen out of the air, and it's everywhere, so when the time comes, all 6.5 billion humans— except the warm ones—will be removed. When I was shown this, it really rattled me: I felt sad for us. But our species is so ghoul infested that we can't survive *en masse* long-term.

So essentially the End of Days is when Gaia is assisted by the Sacred Beings and the reincarnated gods that are now in human form to end it all and bring about a new start. It is the return of Kali, the destroyer.

Okay, we'll leave this for a minute and go back to your advancement and well-being. The end of the world as we know it is all very well, but getting you across the line is more important right now.

THE MALICE OF FOUR THOUGHTS 8

I met a woman from Africa years ago who had very special qualities. There was an inherent beauty in her. She possessed a languid, effortless dignity that was refreshing and unusual. She was ordinary in human terms, and very humble, but she had a spirituality I don't have . . . a grace I know nothing about. She was higher than I was by a few thousand miles.

Naturally I was intrigued. I wanted to learn what made her so special. We worked together on a small project for a New Age promoter, so for a few weeks I saw her every day.

She was raised by ugly parents in a strict, religious family; and because she didn't believe in their religion, she was vilified and mistreated. She had three brothers who bullied her mercilessly; and she married an Algerian man who was an egoist obsessed with himself, who wouldn't work or lift a finger to help, so she went out and worked at a menial job for many years to pay the bills and support him. I asked her if she resented her husband for his indifference and laziness; she did not— she loved him anyway.

I got the impression from her that her husband didn't really pay any attention to her whatsoever except to boss her about. I asked her if that was a problem, being so unloved and unwanted; she said it wasn't. And she loved her parents even though they seemed to be the epitome of the tyrannical Fat Controllers: dark, bigoted, and small-minded. She told me how her father-in-law was a chauvinist racist and hated her. I asked her if it was difficult being in his house, knowing of his hatred for her; she said she didn't mind.

Talking to her, I realized that she had faced discrimination and resentment from people everywhere she went, but for some odd reason, it never bothered her. It never altered who she was. I began to wonder whether she was a hidden saint, an unknown holy person who walked among us. I couldn't work out what was so different about her. She had a very gentle and delicate way about her.

Then it came to me: she was the only person I'd ever met in my life who had no malice. Even though she'd lived a terrible life by the standards we understand, she carried no resentment, no darkness, in her about it. She accepted all the evil around her without one word of complaint.

She taught me a great lesson; it was very humbling, as I've had a certain amount of malice in my heart, because every time I saw injustice in the world, I wanted to rip its throat out. My mother was Sicilian, and there are no Sicilians in heaven as far as I know. So that was a karmic setback for me early on.

I was married to an Australian lady for six years, and her mother was in the Australian Hall of Fame for working-class resentment, bigotry, and racism. She was an inverted snob of an especially virulent nastiness that is common and indigenous in Oz—she didn't really have any redeeming qualities.

I'd lie in bed at night thinking of 30 ways of pushing the ol' bat down the stairs—malice of 30 forethoughts! I felt that I would be doing the world a favor. When I couldn't figure out how to get rid of the grisly cow, I left Australia, and her daughter, as the only other solution. Luckily, I wasn't quite as Sicilian as I thought I was.

We have to suffer injustice, often while it bleeds at our feet, and we have to love the Tao instead, for if we go at it with malice, we rot our soul and suffer a spiritual death.

— I think injustice is our global karma for each of us having been too Sicilian in a past life, and righteous indignation and vengeance score zip; they combined to form the first two of the four malicious thoughts or emotions that we need to avoid: **emotional antagonism** and/or **thoughts of vengeance.**

I was raised in Africa. I detest racists, bigots, and discrimination, but detesting the rednecked racist or the chauvinist pig is also not the way to go, for if we feel like that, we offer the same hate that they find so normal, so that's the second malice to avoid. The world is full of elitist snobs and "chosen ones" and people full of antagonisms and hate. There is nothing we can do about it. At best, we can busy ourselves selling them things that their inflated egos will buy!

— **Jealousy** is the next malice. People are often secretly jealous, and they commonly hate purity and beauty. That's why beautiful women are hated by other women and why people who are very beautiful face much resentment in life, for they inadvertently highlight everyone else's ugliness.

I met a young man in the south of France who was the most stunningly good-looking man I've ever seen. He was in his mid-20s, tall, suntanned, and very well dressed—the symmetry of his face was faultless; he looked like a god to me. I'm not gay, by the way, but I couldn't keep my eyes off him, as he was so beautiful. He seemed from another world. I saw sadness in him that evoked a great pathos in me . . . I knew that his life was hard, for while I'm sure that women instantly gave themselves to him, he lived in a lonely, loveless place of being a sex object and of being too perfect, with all the silent resentments he suffered to go with it. Humans don't like too much beauty unless they can buy it and/ or capture it—it shows them up.

Jealousy is the hidden trait of the inverted snob, like a million Australian plumbers and bricklayers who hate the world because they weren't born upper-class—it's a form of insanity, really—or women who compare themselves to others too much, so they come to hate themselves because their hips are too wide, their nose is too big, or one of their breasts hangs lower than the other. I tell them, "Forget trying to be perfect—it will rot your soul. If your uneven breasts really bother you, lean over a bit and the longer one will come up and both will look the same!"

Comparing yourself to others isn't advisable, for it takes you to dark places, wherein a spiritual death awaits.

— The last of the four thoughts of malice is **rage**— silent or expressed. I said in my other books that all anger comes from contradictions of the ego's opinion. The ego decides that it wants things one way, and life delivers them another.

Often this psychological trait—the insistence of the ego—comes from an unhealthy need to control people and the anger that flows when they resist. Much of it is related to fear and the need to dominate others to feel safe. Some filters through from the demonic. People who get angry quickly are usually narcissistic and egocentric, and that causes anger to flood their feelings in a systematic overload of hate and disdain for anyone who might usurp or belittle them or contradict their inner Nazi. It's a form of hellish, ongoing, perpetual malice.

The trick is to accept life as it comes without fighting it emotionally. No fear, no anger . . . that is what the higher beings taught us.

The lady from Africa who had no malice for the injustice she suffered or the evil of her tormentors taught me a lot. I saw her as a saint.

I am not a saint; I realized that I could learn much from her. I've always had a strong sense of justice, and I rebelled against *in*justice, hoping to right wrongs and set people free—it was the grandiose white-knight syndrome in me, although in a way, I did liberate some people from the agony of their lives with my books and seminars. That liberation was a good thing, but being frustrated by the injustice of the world was a hopeless direction . . . the belligerence of it rotted my soul.

We are required to suffer in silence with dignity and to accept injustice as part of our karma with no adverse reaction or malice. Essentially, we're not allowed to hate people just because they hate *us*. So I will have to come to love my rotten ex-mother-in-law whether I like it or not. Eek!

Certainly, you can act as the white knight from your goodness, but if you do so, be anonymous and silent. Don't use it as a covert system to empower or dry-clean your shadow and rub up your ego or as a way of being seen to be good. We must have compassion for people who have been hurt by injustice, but to be angry and fight the system is futile, as it doesn't allow for a proper understanding of our karma. Gaia will sort it all out in the end; and in the meantime we have to love people, even the evil ones, with grace and dignity, and we have to love and forgive *ourselves*. The last thing we need is any more rancor, since the world is full of it.

The lady from Africa taught me these things. I was very grateful to her, for she redeemed me without ever knowing it. It was the kind, sweet way in which she lived her life that showed me pure grace, and it sent me hobbling over my built-in malice and in the right direction.

THE NEW DIGNITY 9

In a world that is degrading in its moral standards and in the treatment of others, we seek to discover a new dignity—not a pomposity or a grand, vainglorious stance, but a silent composure that speaks of one who is strong and well versed in his or her understanding of the eternal Tao and the way energy delicately ebbs and flows. I've discussed the absence of malice and how if we seek to achieve real composure, we have to detach from the insidious nature of the mind that protests every little setback and takes up the cudgel of indignation for every situation we're in.

I was taught by the higher beings that the torment of the innocent isn't our individual responsibility. All must grow and learn through their karma and work their way out of the difficulties they get into. People must be allowed to process their pain. It sounds brutal, but that's the only way they grow spiritually. And *yes,* this applies to you. You have to become mature, sort your situations out, and suffer your karma without grumbling. This is the new dignity you can acquire.

To arrive in the transdimensional world of the misty Lake of Avalon, you have to be finished with the affairs of man and their struggles of light and dark, blame and recrimination. It stands to reason that to transcend, you have to go past human things, human concerns, and you must process your pain and resolve it and fall to silence—as a settled human whose mission has been completed. Then you'll step out of the ghoul evolution of humans into the magical world of the Aluna animals that can talk and think and act in magical ways, that react to love and soft emotions—animals that work tirelessly to bring about the Renewal that lies up ahead.

It is a fairy-tale dimension of mythical Tao-beings— ones that await you. Grace awaits . . . the celestial goodness is there for you to accept and embrace if you wish, as is the miracle healing . . . it is all there. This is not a myth—it is all *real* and here right now in our solid reality for you to stumble upon.

The world of the Tao-beings is a real one, just as our world is real; the Avalon lake is at a real location, only a mile or so up and over the little green hill that stands in the lands behind the pub; and the Camelot arches that are placed in the forests and in other locations (some are in cities) are also real to see. I've been to 30 so far.

The multidimensional celestial world has gradually threaded its way into ours like the fingers of God interlocking with those of our frail human hand, weaving the speckled ambience of the Aluna through our soul. This interlocking of the dimensions will save us and allow us to evolve to become beings of pure light. Essentially, you can enter into your next incarnation as a Light Being without having first died in this one.

To "arrive" implies a journey that anyone can take, like a taxi ride from the railway station, but to understand it properly, you have to substitute the words *be the same as* instead of the verb *arrive*. So to arrive at the Camelot arches, you have to "be the same as" the arches. To see a hundred stags from the Aluna shoulder to shoulder on the shores of a moonlit lake, which we have seen, you have to "be the same as" a hundred stags, with the same silent majesty—the same power, profundity, dignity, and serenity. To see the Lion of Judah face-to-face inches from your nose so that you can even feel its breath on your skin, you have to have the same courage and bravery, the same agility, the same breathtaking dignity as the lion.

With a new dignity, you shift your mind from traveling *toward* where you might want to go, and striving endlessly to get there, to becoming instead "the same as" the place you'd like to find yourself in. It is an ambient resonance in your heart, not a residency that's established by arriving someplace. It's very subtle.

The bearing of decorum and serenity we hope for takes a while to achieve, but we have time; and the grace I speak of is an outcropping of a silent, spiritual nobility that seeks little for itself, one that is settled and neutral toward all things, toward all matters as they arise. It is the settled heart that so few possess—humans who don't rush about hither and thither, raise their voices, or act coarsely . . . those who don't need to exert themselves in the company of others, who can listen without speaking, who are happy to take the last place, happy to wait through all eternity if need be. It's the heart that beats in time with all the collective hearts of multidimensional hyperspace, both human and nonhuman, rather than the solitary human one that beats only to its ego's desires.

The new dignity is incorporated in a delicate aestheticism, which is sometimes described as a "critical appreciation and reflection upon art, culture, and the natural world." It is the world of refined judgments, sentiments, and taste. We say it is the soft eye of men and women of distinction who see beauty in the philosophy of art and the subtlety and refreshment of nature—the aesthetics of the polymath: a person who has an intrinsic eye for beauty and can command skills in many a field, be it painting, architecture, sculpture, music, or design.

The multitalented polymath is a person like blessed Hildegard of Bingen, a German abbess in the 1100s who founded several monasteries. She was also a writer, linguist, scientist, philosopher, herbalist, poet, and visionary. She is thought to have been the founder of modern opera, and she was the first woman who wrote about the female orgasm. She was also an accomplished painter. Her whole life was an example of pure information as an inspiration from the celestial.

And of course, Leonardo da Vinci, who is known as the Renaissance man, is the most famous polymath. His dignity and reverence for God and his eye for beauty took him to pure information that no one had at that time, so he drew helicopters and submarines 400 years before they were finally invented. The dignity of his aestheticism carried him head and shoulders above all others. It is the detached dignity that comes from a respect for beauty and the love of the feminine spirit that opens the doors of creativity for you.

The settled heart of the newcomer to this dignity spreads out far and wide, for it thinks and feels as few humans can. Such people can see because they're not cluttered by the madness of the mind and its emotional reactions; rather, they're settled and linked to higher information and a dignified calm. The settled heart soon sees that it has few needs it cannot provide of itself, so that gives it a selfless decency.

When people aren't leaning on others etherically or emotionally, this equitable stance lends them an intrinsic width that you could describe as the breadth of their etheric field (its sideways motion). Remember that the traumas and needs of the ego are vertical. So in serenity, the width of a person's logo is carried naturally outward toward the celestial, which, you know, follows the same sideways path or direction as the transverse wave of light that's placed at 90 degrees sideways to the normal path of light.

The narrow mind installs a constrained, tight energy around a human—it travels nowhere, or it travels down the dull conformity of a tick-tock life, parroting what others are parroting. It is a facet in the dull mind of a collective normality. The person's inability to create new ideas comes from the mind's inability to go wider, to become original, so it falters. In fact, etherically, it attempts to suck energy from others to sustain itself and achieve more elevation. Soon one falls back into a false entitlement, feeling others should sustain one. To radiate silently is dignified; to pillage is not so.

Certainly, we have to pay rent, raise children, and arrive at work on time . . . but we must learn to do all these things without falling off balance and losing ourselves and our dignity in the struggle. By walking slowly and deliberately through life in a calm and centered way, with as much grace and dignity as possible, we arrive without moving very far, if at all. It is undignified to struggle and lean into people, demanding things, to tussle to win their affection and acceptance, or to fight to get them to act in certain ways they're often incapable of.

Struggle and confrontation will drag you down. So, instead, smile on them and their weaknesses, and laud their every success while praying for their good fortune and well-being. That's why it's important to walk in the rhythm of the heartbeat of Gaia, to be sustained and taught by that, and to have all your desires tempered so that in your clarity and simplicity, you lack for nothing, as there's nothing much you want.

The dignity I speak of isn't hard to achieve, but you do have to let go. You fought the good fight, marching under the blood-red banner of your emotions and indignations; and you shunned evil, often reacting to it, not realizing, perhaps, that you were only ever looking at an outer manifestation of yourself and *your* darkness.

What justice do we really seek? What pleasure will a hollow victory or vengeance over human evil really offer? To struggle to be better than the hopelessly weak or the indolent—or to be more handsome than the gnarly, narcissistic face of humanity—is of no great achievement. Squeaky-clean is irritating, like fingernails grating on a blackboard; and anyway, the pretense of it serves no purpose, for none of us is spiritually ever much more than various shades of dull gray. Besides, the "squeak-squeak" of squeaky-clean is like hungry mice scurrying along the baseboards of your sentiments and aspirations, keeping you awake at night judging yourself in the light of others and worrying.

Let the banner of your protest drop from your blistered hand . . . and in that way you will have two arms free with which to embrace humanity and allow the new dignity to carry you beyond the world of the mundane, justice and injustice, and the vicissitudes of a poorly understood karma.

In the end, the only triumph is to return home, and the eternal Tao is the compass we use to grant us the resonance of that safe return. The Tao is woven into the souls of the animals, and without them to guide us, we can't arrive at the celestial, for they are its keepers.

GRACE AND THE MAGICAL ANIMALS 10

Very early on, we began to see the magical animals and birds in the Aluna: the white tiger, jaguars, the white lion, the white zebra, the white owls, the white giraffe, eagles, brown and black bears, wolves, and many more. The magical animals are very highly evolved; they're usually associated with protection, like the black panther, for instance, that often appears with a golden snake around its neck. Sometimes the animals are linked to knowledge. When the owls open their wings, there are 16 dimensions held there that they command. That's 13 more than we see, and we hardly command *our* 3 at all.

The first animals that come to you are usually the dogs, as they come to guard. At the same time you may feel a cat walk over your bed at night, or it may snuggle up. That is an Aluna cat: a real cat, we would say, but not a physical one in 3-D.

Then, of the magical animals, the wolf usually comes or appears to you first—which is odd because in the wild the wolves have survived by being very elusive, and skittish of humans.

Next people usually see the bear. It represents great power. I had an odd etheric sensation of feeling brown for a few days: half-brown but not totally brown. It was mysterious; then I realized that the brownness was fur. It was the bear. I'd etherically merged with the bear half-and-half. It has never left.

The magical animals can fry your logic "over easy"— you soon go to egg-yolk mush, double quick. You just have to believe and pray for protection and they come. There is much love for us even though we have treated them so badly.

One evening in a hotel in Vancouver, I saw a fully grown white tiger in the bedroom of my suite, sitting in the doorway. I was rather alarmed. I wasn't expecting it. It's odd to see a wild animal in the room with you; it fried my noodles a bit. It was on the floor on the carpet, with one leg across the front of its body. It stayed there in the bedroom for more than an hour, after which I lost sight of it. There was a big fight in the Aluna at the time—that's why it came.

Not all the animals fight and protect—the bear and the wolf do; and the cat is a fighter, as is the scorpion, which can fly through the Aluna and sting someone in 3-D. Then the rest of the animals are guardians or keepers of dimensions and doorways, and they have much information about humans and the human condition.

The animals are side by side with us in the Aluna; they speak and learn and evolve to become more. So, for example, the white tiger might evolve to enter the soul of the owl—and vice versa—so each might learn the strength and wisdom of the other. We saw one animal that was half lion, half peacock. It was difficult to comprehend but very beautiful. Nothing is static . . . it's all evolving all of the time, trying to go higher or degrading to a lower state.

Call to the power and wisdom of the animals in prayer—it will rocket your comprehension of things. Worship Gaia and grace flows from the intense oscillation of her violet heart, and it flows to you effortlessly. You can't make it to the Camelot dimension without the animals, as they're the guardians of the door—almost no one knows that fact, but it is true, vital.

Do this: Get pictures of animals and put them on a bedside table and look at them for a few minutes before you go to sleep. Try to enter into the soul of each animal; call to them to come out of the Aluna toward you, and ask for protection. When you meditate, place a mental image of each of the animals around you in a complete circle so a ring of their power surrounds you. Blow three soft breaths of love on each one. These ideas help you.

THE
SHIMMERING
DOOR

11

Thirty years ago my old teacher spoke of the dimensions of Camelot and the Camelot doorway, and he spoke at length of the Taoist sages and their nonassertive ways of effortless action and tenderness, as well as their love of nature, which he said was the key to multidimensional experience because it encapsulates a delicate comprehension of grace.

Then he said, "Tolerate everything and skim the lake," meaning we should accept life and purify ourselves constantly, and he said we should search for the hidden door. My teacher was a strange man—he was decades ahead of his time. I owe him a great debt. He didn't say where that door was or how we should search, but it was obvious what he meant: *process your life and journey inward to discover who you really are.*

I took to these instructions and never wavered, although there were times when the exigencies of marriage, family, and a tick-tock life kept me greatly engaged elsewhere. I found the door in the end, the same one Castaneda found—we know that for sure now—and so will *you* find it if you take to the same instructions, follow exactly, and are dedicated. It won't take you 30 years—3 to 5 at the most, for we are now in the endgame and things are going much more quickly.

The door shimmers with a celestial intensity that's not easy to describe. I must say, I always thought of it as a regular door with hinges and a doorknob, but it's not like that at all. It's an oblong box several yards wide at its entrance and maybe two and a half yards high, with an unknown length going inward. It looks like a box constructed as a geometric curtain, made of pentagons that are silver and white; essentially, it's a transdimensional anomaly like the others I've talked of before—a portal at the threshold to other worlds, like that of Castaneda's world of the midnight wolves. It is extraordinarily beautiful.

When I saw it form itself in front of me, it stretched right across the hotel room I was in. I could see that it had depth. It goes inward quite a long way—more than four yards at least. I couldn't see the other end of it, but I did see a wolf right in the middle, guarding it. The wolf isn't the only one that performs that duty, so I've been told, as other animals guard it from time to time, but I haven't seen them as yet.

Without question, the Shimmering Door is one of the most celestially magnificent things I have ever seen. I first saw it at 2:15 P.M. Pacific time on December 22, 2007; it was with me for more than seven hours, until 9:45 that night. Its radiant light shimmers at a pulse that oscillates at four cycles a second, so it is the same pulse as the theta brain wave.

As the doorway—which is the entrance to the Camelot dimensions—shimmers, it creates a concussive effect on one's body and one's etheric. It touches your heart creating a *donk-donk-donk* effect that impinges on you 240 times a minute. Multiplied over the time that it was with me that day, it came to 108,000 pulses or oscillations. As those donks touch your feelings and your soul, they change you very deeply. You become less human and less solid, and you feel yourself carried away to a magical higher world.

The pulse of the Camelot entrance is extremely intense, and at first it rather scared me. Furthermore, it dominates the room so much that one can't really see the edge of the walls or the furniture very well at all—everything shimmers at the same pulse. In fact, I found it quite hard to keep my eyes open for any great length of time, as the concussive effect made me feel rather queasy. The whole room I was in wobbled at the same four cycles a second. It took me many hours to get used to it enough to where I could stand up and walk about a bit.

When the donk-donk of the shimmering curtain touches you, it wobbles your legs—you don't feel that you have much control of your muscles—and when you stand, you sometimes have the sensation of being pulled backward. I nearly fell over several times. I can see now why it will take some very experienced, solid adults to get the children across. The kiddies will find it very magical, but without an adult to reassure them, they would be very scared; they couldn't make it.

Beyond the doorway are more celestial heavens, the ones I've always promised in my books, like the lush worlds that I know quite well. This is where some of us come from. The greens are very green, and the flowers very bright and colorful—they flourish in a radiance that doesn't exist here. And the interior ambiences of the lush worlds are romantic, much like the furnishings of the Belle Époque era. It is all very lush and romantic, and the beings in that beautiful world have the same sensuality and romanticism as their surroundings: it's intrinsic to their energy.

We discovered, to our amazement, that humans who transcend to these other worlds, such as the lush one, have romantic commitments—partners they love—and they have a sexual life. They give birth to children, just as we do on Earth, except the children are born to the lush world and don't have to work hard and know things to get there.

We also discovered that the higher gods procreate, making love and creating new energy that goes out across vast dimensions and the entire universe. It is the orgasm of the female gods that grants us breath. For this Universe may be plasma and atoms and carbon and solid planets, but it all came from the Goddesses' orgasm, even if it looks real and solid and scientific to us. The entire Universe began first in another dimension as a nonsolid cloud of the Great Goodness, which was ejected from the heat, power, and love of a vast female being—beyond comprehension, really—a being who knew she was making a new universe when she took her consort to her breast.

The big bang was an orgasm. Note that I'm not saying the big bang was *like* an orgasm—it actually *was* one. The male orgasm is wet and sticky, and it doesn't have the power of the female's, but she needs his divine love and his penetration of her to complete the correct fractal codes that will allow the universe to prosper in its correct mathematics and for life to form eventually. Essentially the Goddess is the mother of all things.

So our rather clunky, sweaty lovemaking is the beginning of a great power that we will learn to use eons from now. All the celestial beings procreate as far as we know.

In my other books I wrote about a being that appeared to me seven years ago that taught me, with visions, almost all I know about the inner worlds. Nearly everything she ever taught me has now been corroborated, with the exception of the very latest new information. The name I gave her was She-She-La-La. She is a goddess-fawn, and she has three children that she has shown us: three little fawns with hooves and fur to the waist and a human's body up from there. Her children are charming beyond words.

The manimals make love, as do the unicorns; and the white lion became white because lions in another dimension made love and raised their energy to become "more," so a new white animal was born. Did you know that if a female human is very pure inside her energy and she embraces the Tao so that she *is* the Tao and is the embodiment of love, she can give rise to a new species of flower that can come from just one of her orgasms? Like this universe, the flower is created by her love and her heat. Extraordinary!

The Shimmering Door is also pure love. It eventually holds the potential for you to rise up to become a Light Being that radiates with the same light as the sun. We are so small in how we think and what we're normally allowed to know. Do you see now how dogma might have inhibited you?

When the curtain of pentagons appeared, a unicorn came very early on. I'd never seen a vision of one before. Unicorns are in a dimension that is like a mystical forest (the She-She people are in there with them)—intense beauty and the eternal Tao is their home. At night they sleep in flowers that are as large as a small cottage. They neigh like horses do, except their sound is very musical;

it is partly a horse's neigh and partly the call of a nightingale. I'd never thought of unicorns and sound before. The neigh is emitted as the sound of their bliss.

It's all real, y'know? Here's why: Humans don't really have original thoughts—they rework old ideas, improving them or understanding them better and better. For a human to invent something, it must already exist in the Aluna, because the human mind has no way of inventing what it has never seen before or knows nothing about. So one or more of the following must be true of people who write fairy books about unicorns:

1. They must have been to those magical worlds in their dreams.

2. Their mirror-self in the Aluna has been into those magical dimensions.

3. They originally come from those worlds.

Otherwise, they would not know to write about this topic at all . . . or to paint it, as Josephine Wall does.

So whatever humans paint, invent, or build is a remake of a preexisting idea or structure in those inner worlds, established artifacts—sometimes very technological and very ancient—that often preexisted this universe and are already formed and in use in the inner hyper-verse of dimensions upon dimensions. Our Universe is small, and there are trillions of universes and probably trillions of dimensions. So a form of the modern iPod would have existed for billions of years before Mr. Jobs of Apple Computer invented it here.

So that's why I say it is all real, as it all exists somewhere. It has to. Even a person who is quite mad who sees gremlins with wings coming through the wall is still seeing a real thing. We know that in the Aluna there are gnarly gremlins with wings, as we've fought with them in the past. So if something is in the human mind, then that "something" exists in one of a trillion dimensions somewhere. We know that now. How that preexisting information trickles down to us is via downloads, as I've said. And they come to us as we go toward them, improving ourselves.

Be diligent and work hard . . . nothing is cast in stone. You can move up anytime—and very quickly—if you so desire, and then of course, you can falter. Nineteen people I know, people I've taught, found the door, and the numbers are climbing fast, so it *can* be done. How many will walk out of this world, as Castaneda did, I can't say, but once you find the door, there is little stopping you.

Of course, many may manage to find the Camelot door but be unable to sustain it when they get there— it is most intense, as I mentioned. I can't say the final numbers—I just don't know—but I *can* say that there are many more who are due to arrive and try: steady people with lots of warmth and all possessed of a silent humility . . . people who walked along the banks of the Tao for many years, strong and content inside an eternity that they couldn't see but they could *feel,* and that was enough to carry them and the children home.

THE GODDESS OF A TRILLION UNIVERSES

12

After I saw the Shimmering Door, I of course had a lot of questions . . . it was all so incomprehensible. A celestial being of immense power, radiance, and luminosity came back four days later to explain it to me. I was grateful. I never expected that.

The Sacred Being was a 40- or 50-foot-tall, intensely beautiful female; she radiated like a god. She stayed for many, many hours—six or more. Sometimes she spoke with a delicate timbre, in a cadence that was very warm and reassuring; sometimes she was silent; and occasionally she showed glorious visions in full color to explain what she was saying.

She began by confirming that the Shimmering Door I saw *is* the entrance to the Camelots that we've all long awaited. She continued by saying that it is the equivalent of the force of one trillion universes, and that it's made from love, but it is one so vast that there are no proper words to describe it.

I still can't get over the idea of a trillion universes—it scrambles my mind; then again, it helps me to think big. Because of visions I've seen in the past, I've always known that this Universe is very small compared to all the possible universes and/or all the dimensions of inner space. One vision I had was of the Milky Way in my hand, so that gave me the first clue of how small this Universe might be.

She then said that in addition to the wolf I saw guarding the door, the bear also guards it. And at the Lake of Avalon there is a female that we've seen many times, usually standing in a boat. She is very delicate and graceful, and she has a long braid that cascades down the right side of her body. She is known to us as the embodiment of grace; we call her the Lady-with-the-Braid.

The Sacred Being that appeared talked about the door, saying one of the functions of the Lady-with-the-Braid is to guard it. And there is another lady at the lake who seems to us to be part female and part owl, and she is also involved in the safety of the door.

The celestial being that came to explain the door asked me and my friend Udita Chohan, who was there at the time, if we wanted her to show us her world. She gave us three seconds to respond—we quickly said yes.

But as she began to show us, and the pulse-oscillation of her world grew stronger and the eternal love flooded in, it swamped us and our legs turned to jelly. We started to lose track of our sensibilities: we began to faint from love. It was all too much, and we had to ask her to turn the experience down, as we were becoming frightened. We were too little to sustain it for long.

Later, she went on to talk about herself and her world. In doing so, she gave us a great amount of information, mathematical figures, technical knowledge, examples, and visions—too many to recount here. But one thing she said that I found fascinating was that all the animals that have ever been alive, all those currently on

Earth, and all the billions that will be born from them—the sum total of all of the animals ever until the end of time—represents one eight-hundredth (1/800) of her energy.

As I said, the being was vast and very tall, and waves of colored energy that looked like appendages of flowing silky cloth emanated from her, but they were a hundred times more alive and beautiful than a human-made fabric. At the end of the appendages were glorious flowers: they were large; there were 752 in total. Each had seven stamens, which is the male sticky part in the center of the flower that the pollen is on, so 752 flowers times 7 stamens for each one, making a total of 5,264.

She pointed to one stamen among the 752 flowers, saying that it was from that stamen that the Goddess Kali was born—that is to say, the stamen gave rise to the power of Kali. I always thought Kali was as high up in the pantheon of gods as one could get; to realize she was just a small part inside another being caused me great wonderment.

Then the Sacred Being said that it was way more than just Kali, as *all* the Sacred Beings and *all* the Goddesses of the lake and *all* the power of the celestial dimensions came from her flowers. Then, as if that wasn't enough, she pointed to yet another stamen among the over 5,000 of them and said that that particular one was where this Universe of ours originally came from. I found that hard to understand.

She was so vast that we didn't know what to call her. Eventually we came up with the name "The Goddess of a Trillion Universes"; it seems apt and rather lovely. Some of these beings are so immeasurable in their infinite endlessness and grandeur that they defy description. We are small; watching the glory of it evokes awe and humility.

One day, sadly, it will all be gone, but for now the glory of the Sacred Beings and the Camelot door is with us—not because we're so special, but because these are critical times. Many of the things I have written in lessons, articles, and books have been given to me by the higher beings, knowing that some people will respond, and then, most won't. In this way, they define whom they're willing to work with and who represents value to them and who does not. They never waste even a minute quantum of energy. I learned that fact some years ago. You'll get *your* chance if you can agree to follow my suggestions about the Three Graces and if you can muster warmth and humility as acolytes to stand by your side.

THE SYMMETRY
OF PLANTS
AND FLOWERS 13

When I used to facilitate fairy walks with magic mushrooms in the forests of Ireland toward the end of the '90s, I came to see the trees very differently. The Celts grant trees memories, so one particular tree they may say is a healing tree, another is a place to reconcile relationships, still another is good for the cure of mental problems, and so forth. Essentially, the mystical Celts give various trees or groups of them identities and functions. They have a reverence for the trees of the woods and forests that I found most endearing.

In the Aluna, the trees are very real, and every plant seems to have a consciousness, so taking a leaf or a flower hurts it unless you ask its permission. There is a delicacy to it all. Recently, in South America I took a beautiful white trumpet-shaped flower from a datura bush, not realizing that I should have asked permission.

Later I saw in the Aluna that the bush was crying, so I went back to apologize and offered some tobacco at its roots, and I returned the flower to where it wanted to be. It was a lesson learned. I felt very embarrassed. I felt for the flower being separated from its family for no reason at all.

In the Ayahuasca (Aya) ceremonies we do in South America, we always put the most experienced people on the six mats that surround the shaman's table because that area can pose problems for beginners, for when the shaman performs his healings on people, entities and dark influences can fly about. One night I called on the souls of the local *arboles* (trees) to stand in front of those mats and make a line of trees between us and the shaman's healing stool as an added screen of protection.

Six trees came in from the garden and stood in a line tightly side by side in front of us, making a protective wall. Then I forgot about them for a bit, and I continued my journey simultaneously while the shaman's healings were taking place.

Forty minutes later, I heard one of the trees call out, "We are tired. We have ghouls in our leaves—help!"

I felt so sorry for them. I cleared the ghouls for them and thanked them for their protection, and I sent them back out into the woods that surround the property. Trees have a great soul. They are part of the greater symmetry of things, part of the overall memory of things that have occurred; they are the silent record keepers. They are brave—they have the dignity I speak of. Trees die standing up . . . unless a hurricane takes them, of course.

My friend Udita the visionary told me that in her visions she saw that the symmetry of a flower and the plants and trees is the same as that which is in the human body. She said that she watched it all unfold during a two-hour period. Our organs are like flowers, our limbs like branches, and the cells of our skin are like small leaves.

When you think of the point of conception, the human cell divides and becomes two, both in a perfect symmetrical balance, and then four—and then eventually trillions of symmetrical cells that make up a baby's body. There is a perfect symmetry in the balance of human organs and how the body works.

Udita said that she saw a vision of the petals of a flower like a white lotus that turned into the eyes of different animals: deer, tiger, and the like. When we are in the beauty of a celestial symmetry in our feelings and there is humility and serenity in the balance of our lives, then flowers run through our limbs and in our energy field, and Udita told me that she has also seen hummingbirds hover in people's chests. The rivers of the Tao are in our soul, as well as outside of us in the reality that surrounds us.

In the modern world, that delicate symmetry is lost in mass gluttony, egocentric consumption, and a disgusting hatred of animals, expressed as disrespect for nature; or it is lost in the asymmetrical ways of our modern degraded humanity: drugs, drink, porno, thieving, lies, vengeance, bitterness, violence, and the covert and cruel nature of stingy humans pretending to be normal.

Technology gave us better health and some financial benefits, but it rotted our collective soul. We became loveless drones in front of screens, with no feelings; and of course, technology empowered our closet-fascist leaders in their surveillance and control over us. It was a dismal failure.

We went to hell because of it, for we fell collectively to an asymmetrical bend that is the antithesis of Gaia, that assails her delicate nostrils like foul air rising from a swamp. She is required to abandon each of us to our fate, as approaching any closer degrades her patina, making her quite unwell. The disgrace and abuse we placed on the feminine spirit, and how we treated women and soft sensibilities, caused the feminine spirit great pain in her deepest soul—wounds so deep that they may never heal—and that pain is the agony of Gaia. It is her disgust.

If you want to turn and go the other way and have the symmetry of flowers in your etheric and in your spiritual logo (identity), then you have to embrace a more rarefied sentiment: one of respect and softness and a true belonging. And that hoped-for belonging has to be in your heart night and day for a while before the disgust that Gaia has had for you melts away and the trees bend over you to embrace you as you pass.

This is how you must now be if you seek to arrive—delicate as a flower and just as beautiful, or even more so. Do this: when you see a beautiful flower, say to it, *Come into my soul, and I will come into yours, and we will teach each other.*

REVERENCE 14

Here is a way to improve the flow of information very fast and change your karma for more grace instantly: develop a stronger reverence . . . it heals you.

Most of my life I have been rather irreverent, although the things I have been irreverent about are the pompous institutions that invite ridicule anyway.

I was raised a Catholic, and I don't have any reverence to offer the Catholic Church; in fact, it disgusts me. It's been estimated that there are 1,000 pedophile priests in the Boston-area Catholic Church alone, which could mean there may be something like 100,000 or more worldwide.

It makes me laugh that they currently want to make the old Pope John Paul II a saint, the man who protected and hid the church's pedophiles for a very long time! Rotten queens run the Vatican, not cheery ones who make you laugh and do a good haircut—wizened old men who violate little boys and sometimes little girls.

And I've always had an utter contempt for the institutions that seek to feed off people and rip them off, much like some churches that are so corrupt.

The reverence I'm suggesting is one for the divine: a reverence for the Goddess, which is linked to the nostalgia for eternity that you may have heard me mention from time to time, which I see as that ancient part of you that remembers that you came from another world, from other dimensions of great light and beauty, that part of you that longs to go home. You should talk to that nostalgia and nurture it with softness and delicate ways—and discipline. And you should tell it that you're trying in every spiritual and human way to return bit by bit . . . so as to build its confidence in order that you may later evoke that relationship (love) you have with the nostalgia . . . so that it will truly carry you home. This technique works.

Society doesn't teach reverence. It teaches boxed ideas that subjugate people, enslaving them. Cold rules—nasty stuff like tax forms, supporting the system without question, turning a blind eye, not rocking the devil's boat, and so on.

We've had enough of all that load of old cobblers! Kali has returned, and she'll sink the bloody boat! None of the religions survive in the end except the Hindu. I found that very odd, but it's true. I know little about Hinduism, and I'm not here to promote it, but it is a fact in the Aluna that it's the only religion that survives. There is a special reason for it—I'll explain later.

Boxed ideas are cruel. They don't come from the heart; they usually come from the need to conform and/ or to impose control from above. How many rules set you free?

Rule 1: Laugh, make love, keep 100 percent of the money you earn, plant a vegetable garden, and be nice to your mother.

Rule 2: Always sing when it rains.

Rule 3: Never read the papers or watch the government's news. I wish, eh? Parrots, man, parrots—brain-dead parrots squawking the covert Nazi agenda. Never mind the white shadow talking on behalf of God, what about those who pretend to help humanity while inflicting the Fat Controllers' agenda?

Rule 4: On September 24th (Stuie Wilde's birthday), anyone caught slapping a traffic warden around will not be prosecuted; instead, they will get a nice chocolate cake courtesy of the National Health Service, which seeks to promote mental health among the citizens, and a day off with full pay, to boot. Nice. Don't you love Stuie's rules? I've become fond of them over the years— *very* fond.

I was in a small American town wandering around barefoot at 3 A.M. when I came upon a group of young lads—teenagers—outside a 7-Eleven. They looked a bit dejected. The police were cruising the streets harassing them for crimes against humanity like walking about and talking . . . stuff like that. I told the boys that they shouldn't let the coppers humiliate them and they should demand that the cops love them and protect them. "Insist on it," I said.

I asked one of the lads to get me a Coke from the store; there was a cop car parked to my left. I stuck the entire contents of the Coke bottle in the petrol tank of the vehicular transport used by the local constabulary conveniently parked nearby. That is why they're called "convenience stores": you don't have to trot around endlessly to cause mayhem. When I first saw the film *Fight Club*, I thought it a biography of my life. Funny, eh?

It cheered the lads up to no end. I suggested they do the same, but they weren't quite mature enough for that kind of caper . . . ya know what teenagers are like? They take time to believe in themselves. It's something to do with hormones and getting laid. Just love them lots— that usually works.

Rule 5: Rule 5 isn't really a rule; it's more a travelers' advisory. "Coke®. Don't leave home without it."

A great teacher of mine once said, "Embrace contentment." For if you don't embrace contentment, then the winter of your discontent is never made summer, as one of Shakespeare's characters suggested it might be. From contentment, reverence flows effortlessly, and that reverence catapults you forward . . . not necessarily to a completely karma-free life, but lighter. ("Oy vey! Whadda you want already for just $15.95?")

Reverence has to be intrinsically woven into your soul. Try kneeling on a stone floor, hands together in prayer—any prayer. Waffle if you're nervous; just practice the position five minutes at a time. You have to become humble. Modern humans suffer from an obesity of the soul. They are too grand, too fat; or they suffer from false entitlement, which is often a shadow trait whereby you elevate your utter irrelevance to some invisible podium for conquering heroes and medal winners—a fashion catwalk, maybe.

Try to see that as one among six-and-a-half billion people, you're totally immaterial to the overall success of the human condition. If you embrace the concept of your irrelevance, it sets you free—free from holding up your ivory tower, free from importance.

Become nothing . . . that's what I tell those poor unfortunates who are keen on the "plank on head" system I use to teach those who study with me. Once you agree to be nothing, you can avoid ego trips and go wider and become everything—in silence, of course. Reverence helps cure your soul of its obesity, which most don't understand is the prime source of their bad luck and disease. Jot that down.

Gaia, as you may know, is the name given by James Lovelock to the overall intelligence of the planet, which is seen as a highly sophisticated organism with the ability to self-correct imbalances in its climatic and biological systems. We view Gaia as a Goddess inside or as part of the eternal Tao. One way in which she attempts to fix things is to gently regulate humans with useful messages.

So, for example, if you overconsume, the wisdom of Gaia might lead you to magazine articles that suggest a simpler, more organic lifestyle: a cottage in Provence . . . that kind of thing. She might hint that you drink licorice tea, as it's an appetite suppressant. If you're very arrogant, and unaware of the harm you create, Gaia might steer you into a humiliating defeat, so you learn.

The system is intelligent. It seeks to take you to a place that hurts you and the planet less, toward low consumption, less activity, and balance. People who are extremely overactive and burn too many resources drop dead of heart attacks, and obese humans almost all die prematurely. It's not the vengeance of Gaia; it's just her protection of self. Prolific consumers who have no care for her lose a hundred grand on the stock exchange to slow them up a bit.

What we call accidents are just Gaia's minor adjustments—tweaking the cogs. That's why the consumers' economy is bound to go broke in the end, as Gaia has to rein in the world's consumption. Maybe a meteor lands in the Atlantic and rubs out New York . . . who knows?

Reverence is a hands-on thing—or in the case of obesity and chocolate, hands-off! You have to get active and make changes so you look convincing to Gaia. I like to say that it is *reverent* action. Sometimes it's just a moment of silence or stopping to look at a flower. I make the sign of the cross because of my Christian background. It's a momentary link into the Sacred Beings and the celestial dimensions we came from as we move through the day, touching back to our spirituality from time to time.

You're always being watched, observed. In the Aluna worlds, you can go from looking like a celestial being to a ghoulish one very quickly. It's a lot to do with how you feel right now, so it's a lot to do with the mark of respect you offer as you go along. It is today's moving prayer as you pass gradually from dawn to dusk.

Reverence is empathy for the Tao, and that keeps you safe—protection builds. If you're mugged in the street for your wallet, it's hard to see that that infringement upon you is linked to your underlying disrespect and disdain for humanity, but it is. Pomposities spawn thieves and disease, and ghouls nibble ya toes at night, tormenting your dreams.

That empathy for gentility is the connection to lighter things: laughter, connecting to humans you trust, swimming at night by the light of the moon, speaking to the animals—tenderness. It's an alliance to nature, a real connection in your feelings, not just one in your head. It's the grand alliance where long ago we all agreed to fight as one.

Once you remember and reestablish that alliance, if you haven't already done so, it will help carry you along. More animals will turn up from the Aluna. Big cats with paddy paws just walk out of their world into this one—you'll find a panther guarding your door for you and your family. We've seen these animal protectors hundreds, if not thousands, of times. They are real. It is all real. It comes from their love for us and the alliance born of the terms of endearment you offer all living things.

The opposite of empathy is disdain. It is graceless. It comes from a silent hatred for humanity, and it often involves indifference for the celebration of life. It hides in your competitive nature, your need to win, your need to dominate situations. If you empathize with people, you don't have to be above them or beat them at anything—agree to lose if need be. There's never a reason to be first; that attitude is an utter embarrassment to your soul.

When you learn not to have to win, you are free. By becoming competitive, you put yourself in a beastly space, like the Olympians or footballers—ego trips: "Me, me, me . . . look at my erection . . . I'm number one." (*Big thingy, small brain,* I reckon.) Agree to be last—that's best, much safer.

To raise your energy, you may need to review your disdain, to look and see and observe yourself being ridiculous. Your soul will cry in its great relief if you ever really look properly. Spirituality is the act of becoming ever more normal, real, and genuine; often in posing and pretending, we get carried away to perdition.

When I watch people in the street, say, disdain is the most obvious to see—it's on their lip. We say it is a cruel lip, thin and curled downward sometimes. Hate is in people's eyes as a slimy patina; arrogance is under their nose between it and the upper lip, and in people's puffed-up chests. The desire for sex is in the surreptitious rocking of their hips or how women rub their thighs unconsciously. Violence is sometimes in the fist, and it's always in the corner of the eye—as an untreated insanity.

People who suffer from overthinking, a narcissistic obsession with self, talk a lot . . . and they go gray, their etheric looks cloudy, their pallor changes, and they get sick as their mind disconnects from grace while insisting on *self*. The way it falls in love with itself and its endless churning eventually irritates them into hypochondria, which is a disease of self-importance.

Shame is seen in a curled-in etheric field—I call it the "kick dog" look—and it's sometimes seen as a dip in one shoulder, usually on the right, as it responds to left-brained thinking and churning. The left side of the brain operates the right side of the body, and vice versa. Shame is also seen, of course, as a lowered head.

And almost all the humans you ever see in the Western world look etherically dirty. Even if their clothes and appearance are spotless like they've just walked out of the dry cleaner's, they *feel* dirty. Some have dirty mouths. A dirty mouth is when people have a lot of lies to tell or when they're very spiteful. You can see their venom in their etheric. Mostly the cloudy dirt around people is disrespect, a belligerent indifference for the divine.

Such a thing calls the ghouls to come and make you sick, to torment your dreams to rattle your stability. They infringe on you as you silently infringe on others.

The irreverence of obesity is obvious to see: it often hangs as unprocessed fear. You can see it as fat in their yellow eyes. It's usually the disease of killers, as one can often see thousands of animal carcasses in the person's belly—the agony of those creatures' deaths linger as a foul karma.

It's really scary to watch these frightening levels of indifference and callousness in the act of satisfying self. It's a death sentence for the soul, as obese people can't ever escape their irreverence, for it walks around with them and disgusts the spirits with every step.

If you want to avoid Gaia's ire, you have to tackle obesity in every form: food, alcohol, drugs, too much talking, too much activity, too much consumption, too much shouting, too many emotions, too much noise, too much nastiness, and so forth. To be in harmony with Gaia, you should consume as little as possible and make do with only a few possessions—tools you need for work, say—and not much else.

To become safe, develop respect as a whispered prayer from your soul. Make it a part of how you walk about and feel every day; put it in your overall energy as a stamp on your logo. Talk softly, have a soft eye for humanity and animals, be polite and don't trash other people's space, stand to one side, have reverence for all— who they are and what they're going through—as their feelings are real for them.

I've always said that one of the great comprehensions in life is never to interfere. A reverence for people's lives and feelings, their pain and difficulties, must be allowed; even if you don't agree, you have to allow people to go through all that.

Reverence isn't fixing everyone. Rather, it's acknowledging that their feelings are important; that what flows from their emotions is important and ought to be listened to; that what they're experiencing is real, to be comprehended and understood; and that the lesson of their pain is that of the Bodhisattva of Compassion. Become like her. Have reverence for all humans, laud their success, encourage them, admire them, and seek to learn from each one of them, not lord it over them. And don't try to fix everything for them.

Silently bless everyone you meet. It helps you. In making their humanity okay and special, you correct yours, for the humility of the Tao is selfless and charitable and often invisible. The greater part of it exists in the Aluna and is rarely seen . . . it is vast.

Then, too, some of its power is here. It's the warm south wind; it's the acorn that breaks open while making no sound. It's the song of the flowers in the early morning that sing tunes almost no one ever hears except them; it's the tender emotions of the way animals care for their young; it's the affectionate embrace that the Tao places around your shoulders, that same embrace that you should offer to others because you love them and because you seek to become like the Tao and like water that takes the lowest spot.

You seek to see and become more. Pray for that: pray to see and become more. Reverence is way more powerful an aid than people know. It is way better than locks and stingy protection devices, burglar alarms for misers.

You need a reverence for people's assets and for their well-being—you're not allowed to hurt them, short-change them, or rip them off. If you trash their property, you have to replace it; empathy will not allow for shoddy dealings. Your interactions must be squeaky-clean at all times, without exception, even if it costs you extra. It's better to be fair than to rot your soul and bring misfortune upon you and your family.

In the end, it's a tender care for the sensibilities of others—to paraphrase Jesus, "Do unto others as you would be done by them." None of these messages ever got old. Irreverence is really an ego trip; selfishness is at its base core. It doesn't help you.

Sometimes in my mind I go to a place in Ireland that I consider my spiritual home. I see myself kneeling there by a lake, and I say some words of thanks for the abundance of people in my life and the gift of being allowed to teach others. And while going to that place in my mind, I enter into the energy of our mother creator Goddess and my reverence for her.

Most of my regular readers know about my quest for the Lady of the Lake, which I wrote about in my book *God's Gladiators*. I gave up looking in the end, but then later, to my great blessing, *she* found *me*. She came for me because I'd searched for her, because I'd loved her faithfully for decades without knowing her, and because of the reverence I had in my heart. She had an extraordinary wraparound digital-fractal eye made of gold circuits. She gave me 15 visions of the destiny of the world, the destruction of Jerusalem being one of them.

It was a big moment for me when she came to find me. She came from her reverence for eternity—like the one I have, albeit mine must be infinitely smaller and less defined. She came back for me from another world. She had a real concern for me, one that is very ancient; and from that encounter with her many magical things happened. She led me to a thousand places, and she introduced me to the fractal worlds and the dimensions, such as 45-up, right, and she showed me the Morph—it arrived just a few weeks later.

Just prior to that time, my body went very hot, and then one of my arms went seemingly translucent. I couldn't sleep or cool down. I'd sit in a cold bath and cool down a bit, but minutes later the heat would come back. It was really frightening and strange. It was an internal heat, not really a body one, so there was no medical remedy.

I couldn't sleep. I was awake for 23 hours a day. The heat burned off the old me and took me up somewhat. It lasted in its most intense form for five months; then I adjusted to it, but it has never gone away . . . it never left me, although I'm used to it now.

The heat comes out of my eyes as two parallel beams of light—it's very uncomfortable to get used to. I think the heat was part of a cathartic transformation from the stupidities of my past when I'd trashed my body doing a bit of obesity of the soul while coping with being young and restless.

Heaven is warm; hell is cold, I kept telling myself as reassurance in the most extreme moments of the experience. Often things happen that we don't understand; one has to learn to hold steady.

Reverence allows for higher beings to appear and help you. It's a great gift if it's bestowed upon you, but they don't come to pump up your importance, to make you rich and famous, or to give you great powers that you might wield over others. They come to help you see the glory of the Tao and the myriad worlds that are just beyond your forearm. Reverence links you to grace and data banks of pure information and the gift of love and creativity. It is like the dignity and respect of a person such as Leonardo da Vinci, his gift, the ability he had to touch the God Force and see and create.

If you mock the celestial and are disrespectful, you do yourself a great disservice. If you have no reverence for your spiritual journey, that's a bad sign. Humans rot and die in agony. There's only one escape from that fate, and only the Sacred Beings can teach you and grant you the blessing of that escape. To insult or ignore your rescuers is foolish beyond words.

Reverence can grant you a teacher like She-She-La-La, or it can send a transdimensional healer to take away a terrible disease or an engineer to help you see. The beings fashion you over time with a new set of eyes: Aluna eyes that are overlaid over your normal ones. The process allows you to see with your normal eyes shut, and it allows for more visions.

There are many beings that have many gifts to offer you. On an Ayahuasca journey once, a tiny little being turned up. He was multicolored, and his body was made up of fractal-digital cubes and geometries. He clamped three prongs on my forehead and started to drill into my skull with a small machine. I questioned him, wondering about it all, saying, "Listen up, Bubba. Are you authorized for this kind of hole-in-the-head drilling caper?"

He didn't answer. He kept on drilling, and then off he went, but his efforts helped me with my Third Eye and perception, so I was most grateful for his abilities and his presence. You don't have to understand things to benefit from them.

Inside a deep reverence is your gratitude expressed in prayer or as a token, an offering you might leave somewhere (at a sacred place, perhaps): a flower you drop in the sea; tobacco you place at the root of a plant; a gold ring you bury, as I did once as an offering to two swans I liked very much (they mate and stay together for life, so the ring was my gift to their marriage, a symbol of it).

To offer gifts is to open yourself up to become more and to attain the attention of spirits that might cast a kindly eye upon you and help you up a bit. The visions all come from another world. They're manufactured and sent down a golden cord that is seemingly flicked through those dimensions to arrive at our minds.

We know little of it and how the mechanism of the colored tubes works, but we can see the four-color videos playing in our minds as short films instructing us minute by minute, showing us how to venerate Gaia in order to learn even more.

In heartfelt gratitude, you're falling backward through *your* humility into the arms of Gaia's, into her protection, as I see it. She cares for her own. Your act of reverence could be just pausing at the bus stop and taking a moment to give thanks for the beauty of arriving; leaning over a flower to admire it; talking to other people's dogs in the street, making them laugh; or watching birds play, encouraging them to fall in love with each other. It is kisses to Gaia when you do it. But it can't be fake—it has to all be presented in the breadth of your inner warmth to have value.

There is an information source around you that walks with you every day in the Aluna; the shamans sing to the beauty of it, and they know how to call it in. I learned by watching them call to the soul of the earth, to the stars above, to the inner worlds. Their reverence for it sends out impulses to these dimensions that are eventually reflected back to them.

I've been in bed meditating many times and seen the celestial light at 45-up, right. I know it's repairing my body, showing me, allowing me to belong ever more. In the end is that not what we all seek: to belong somewhere? We may not have the elevation to belong to the world of the black unicorns, but we can enter in other places and belong where the plump owls dance over the lake, where the full moon lasts 28 days. We can do that.

Carlos Castaneda wasn't a saint by any means—he just had the symmetry of Gaia embossed in his logo; we know that as a fact. It was the symmetry that got him across.

How do we know that? We watched him over there for a while—many weeks, in fact—as the beings showed us his new life and the dimensions he commands a presence in. Then one night he walked in, back in here. Very few humans can go through the Shimmering Door and walk back into this 3-D world. He only said one word, *Hello*, and then he left again less than a minute later—strange but true.

He's linked to the wolves. He called the Aluna the *Nagual*. He knew it well and called to it; that's why he had the power.

Resonate your empathy, carry it around your neck, care, step inside a silent prayer that talks of the eternity and the hyperspace beyond the beyond. From coarse and hard, you move to soft and sweet . . . to a place where you're truly nice, not just pretending to be normal and nice, but *actually* nice: tender in your silent power, a true blessing to all those you meet. As you resonate the power of reverence, it takes you toward Gaia and the Tao. It's a temple of oak trees that bends over to greet you, and the beings will be there to greet you in the clearing.

So entering in a relationship with the divine isn't some pompous rubbish—posing for watchers, meditating cross-legged in the park like some scruffy Buddha. Rather, it's a silent prayer, a resignation to beauty . . . calling to it, caring for it, loving it. It is *you* wrapped in the arms of your nostalgia, ever the child of a multiverse for all eternity, respectful.

THE TENACITY
OF SPIRIT

15

When I first heard of the dimension of Camelot and the hidden door 30 years ago, the idea instantly resonated with me. My former teacher told wonderful stories of the sages of old China and the Tao, and none of that magic ever left me. Even though I hopped about like a flea in a dog show, traveling three million miles and talking to hundreds of thousands of people—and two wives, one child, 19 books, the Morph descending, and the ghoul wars—all of that initial teaching persisted in my concentration. It was part of my soul. Sometimes my dedication was very strong, and sometimes I was more distracted . . . but all in all, nothing ever changed very much.

Eventually, I arrived at the Lake of Avalon, with 18 friends in the line. I was honored to accompany them. Temüjin, who later became known as Genghis Khan, began with a tribe of 17 fighters—one of whom was his mother—so 18 in the line seemed a blessing and a proper good fortune to me.

The journey requires not just reverence but tenacity and a commitment, one that comes from deep within. As I see it, you have to travel "sight unseen," believing in yourself, using your feelings to guide you through a multi-dimensional hyperspace that you're blind to at first. And you have to be mature and understand that the journey can't always be exciting, with many different things happening all the time. There will always be quiet periods, time for contemplation and reflection and time for just being. There will be occasions when it seems as if nothing is happening to you. But things are *always* happening, somewhere, at some level.

The sage must sit in meditation in winter as well as in spring, and the white tiger must hunt when food is scarce as well as when there is plenty—it has to hunt when it's tired as well as when it's energetic. And so, just as the sage cannot choose when he leaves the valley or the white tiger cannot choose not to hunt, *you* cannot choose when things will happen. You have to have tenacity and endurance, and wait.

It's not possible to always make this journey what you want it to be. Whether visions flow or not, whether times are exciting or not, whether there is beauty or sadness, there should always resonate from your heart an endearment with spirit and your respect for the journey. You must exhibit an ability to wait patiently and allow your decision to endure and to be strong and resolute so you demonstrate your journey to be one of silent dedication at all times—a dedication in matters of spirit, a dedication that comes from the depths of your heart.

Don't allow your dedication to be brittle—too greatly reliant on excitement, experiences, and visions. This cannot always be so. There cannot be these kinds of expectations. An unconditional, selfless dedication is the only way. This may seem harsh in the world of rewards, quick fixes, and consumerism; but this is the only way, the true way.

And it is to those who follow this endearing way that the beings and animals look to, for to these people, the journey is a part of their being, a part of their spirit; and therein it sparkles like a bright star in a milky sky. And sometimes that star will move across the heavens, taking those people with it to worlds and places they never dreamed possible—worlds and places that are real, that have always existed at all times; it is the doorways *to* them that are not always open.

This is a most marvelous journey, if you believe in it—always, without expectations. It is a most marvelous journey if you follow the Three Graces and the teachings of the Tao.

For me, I see tenacity as the samurai stance: foot forward, poised, settled, calm, ready . . . even if your knees are knocking in terror. It is 90 minutes' sleep and an entire day's work ahead; it is love beyond how we were taught to love, a celestial care for each other; it is awe in its childlike form; it is the breadth of your expectancy made manifest in each new victory; and it is the birth of the Brave New World that is to arise from the ashes of the old.

THE HELL WORLDS

16

Over the years, I've learned a lot about the ghouls and the hells that they exist in. Some of this I've seen in the Morph, especially the Inner Matrix, which are those inner worlds of hell where the digital-fractal devils dwell, and I also know the beings of the Outer Matrix quite well from fights I've had with the UFOs, and transdimensional entities, like the Men in Black, as mentioned.

But I've also learned of the inner ghoul-worlds through lessons that were taught to me via Ayahuasca. Each of the last 68 sessions with the plant medicine has taken me down into the hell worlds farther and farther. I reckon I've now done just over 500 hours in there—more than 20 entire days of my life! Of course, most people never go to those worlds on Aya, or they go just once to see it and understand it, which helps them, but it was my karma in this life to make the journey downward many times.

Some of the early hell worlds were reflections of my own darkness, so it helped me enormously knowing the nature of who I really was at that time seven years ago and what to expect up ahead. It gave me a shock, and it made me change my ways lickety-split, quick time, pronto. So I escaped from that fate by being able to see. In these matters, I was truly blessed.

But later the hell worlds I went to weren't really anything I could relate to or see in myself. At first I wondered why I was there, but later I understood that I was being trained to withstand those worlds without flinching. They're very ugly and depraved, they feel very dirty, and sometimes they're scary.

Watching them for more than half an hour makes you very sick and nauseated. So I had to learn to get used to the queasy nature of things and not to throw up constantly. Eventually I discovered that if I took a 30-second break every 20 minutes or so, I could endure the nausea for hours and hours.

The ghouls sometimes lie on your belly, and I learned to protect myself and flick them off, but there are always a few too many to handle, so speedy accelerations to the bathroom every 90 minutes or so are part and parcel of doing business down there. There's no remedy for that discomfort.

The hell worlds are layered deeper and deeper, getting darker and darker the farther down you go. Near the top of those worlds are intellectual hell worlds of black imps; they are naked, bony creatures about four to five feet tall. You can see them rather well—there is quite a bit of light in their upper-hell world. The imps are degraded humans that became so because they were the devils of misinformation and tricking people: crooked journalism, Internet fraud, pornography, lies, embezzlement, and deliberate distortions like political misinformation and media hype. There are even imps down there with laptop computers; it is utterly bizarre to watch them.

Below them are the black digital-fractal worlds of the Lords of Cruelty, into which cruel humans descend to be trapped by a fierce power. As you enter the world of the evil lords, a bracket like a parenthesis closes in around you and it traps you—you can't escape. It is a wall around you that you cannot see. It evokes terror as you know you will never get out. That place probably is a hell of no return. I escaped because I was not destined to stay there. I was only there to see that it exists so I could talk about it. It was bloody scary.

Below that area are layers upon layers of digital-fractal ghouls, many of which look almost human except they are deformed and distorted, and they feel very dirty when they get close. They often have silly appendages, crowns and scepters and ego-trip icons like the gilded thrones they sit on, and swords and spears, and medals and regalia that describe their feigned importance in their former human lives.

Those ghouls twist and turn and move constantly, never staying still for more than a few seconds. They are all very angry, and they snarl and growl and spit and make ugly faces hoping to scare you. They are full of jealousy and hate.

The entities number in the millions, maybe billions, but as each ghoul you see is a compilation of many different evils there is no way of telling what the absolute final total might be. It is like those Russian dolls: there is one evil dwelling inside another. They are composites of evil.

I have seen more than 70,000 ghouls degrade (melt). As they do so, four other ghouls of a lesser degradation pop out of the original ghoul, as if they were hiding inside, so one can see what the ghoul used to be before it arrived at its current revolting state of being. And as those other identities also melt away, the last that appears is often an image of the human who originally created the ghoul—its initial instigator—a human who may have lived on Earth maybe many thousands of years ago: a cruel tyrant king, an evil woman, a dark manipulator, or a torturer who flourished in our prehistory. Even degraded Neanderthals and cavemen pop up from time to time, meaning that some ghouls have existed in those hellish worlds I see for maybe a hundred thousand years.

The Neanderthal ghouls are very rare, so I'd say they are an exception. The more plentiful ghouls one sees stretch back no farther than 4000 B.C.—so, back 6,000 years to the empire of Sumeria, which is considered to be the cradle of civilization, based as it was at the confluence of the Tigris and the Euphrates, in what is now modern Iraq. Of course, to see a ghoul that is 6,000 years old boggles the mind, thinking about how much evil and sickness it must have spread over all those years.

I can't say how many ghouls I've seen in total—there would be no way of counting them all, as sometimes they appear in groups of six or eight at a time—but the number is very much greater than 100,000. In order to keep a small part of the Matrix clear, I've been sent to fight them using the cactus needles on my fingers, so I've destroyed many while down there.

In my estimation, they appear out of the gloom at the rate of 5 a minute, and if you multiply that by the 500-plus hours that I've been in their worlds, it would come to a total of 150,000 that I've seen—and the number I've done in and killed is about 70,000. That is more or less an accurate figure, since I did count the ones that went down as I went along. I've done ghouls in for this lifetime!

Every one you see is different, just as every human alive looks slightly different to all other humans, although there are exceptions to the "all different" rule in the ghouls' world.

In the very low, very dark hell worlds below those of digital-fractal, semi-human-looking ghouls in the preceding description are the reptilian worlds. Imagine a very fat anaconda that's miles upon miles long—so long, in fact, that you never find its head; only its body is apparent. Those anaconda beings all look the same, and also in there is a form of crocodile-ghoul that is very similar to all other crocodile-ghouls that exist in those very dark, dank worlds.

There is also a type of large rodent with a very long snout like an anteater, and all those long-snouted rodent-ghouls look pretty much alike. They remind me of the paintings of Hiëronymus Bosch. The reptile-ghouls are all similar, just as animals of a species might look more or less the same; only the human-looking ghouls are all different.

Just as a human may be slightly evil and then progress to more and more nastiness, the digital-ghouls seem to degrade over time, becoming less and less human looking. Sometimes they drift to grotesque digital forms that are vaguely human in shape, as they might have the rudiments of a face, but they're so far from being a person that one can hardly recognize any humanity in them. And some are hybrids: part animal, part bird. Imagine a hideous human face—angry, cruel, and ugly— with the long, sharp beak of a bird of prey instead of a nose, and scales instead of skin. Some are piglike; and many are part reptilian, part human.

I think the hybrids come about because the reptilian section of the human brain/mind mechanism is cold and cruel. So humans who live their lives devoid of feelings are almost entirely in the reptilian brain—maybe that's why they wind up in the hybrid state.

The ghouls can shape-shift, so sometimes they can appear in the hell worlds as a cute little kitten or a cuddly lion cub, but if you look carefully, you'll see that the symmetry of the animal they're pretending to be soon breaks up. The cute kitten goes demonic looking—you see the true nature of what's behind it—and a horrific ghoul emerges out of it.

Sometimes the ghouls attempt to copy people you know so that you'll trust them when you see them. They may take the form of a parent or a much-loved sibling, but always the symmetry breaks if you stare long enough, so they can't really trick you. One ghoul attempted to trick me by pretending to be a church bell. Ding-effin'-dong—no chance!

The function of the ghouls is to degrade humans who are still alive, inhibit plant growth, and spread disease; and then some specialize in psychological ploys that make people weak and easily addicted to debilitating habits. They spread fear and despondency, distrust and confusion, and some of what they do is to propagate the currency of hate. There are specific ghoulish entities linked to certain religious and political ideas, and others that are in charge of spreading one disease or another.

Down there I once bumped into a caterpillar-looking ghoul that had metal scales protecting it like little shields. I heard the word *meningitis,* and from its mouth came two mosquitoes that carry the disease. For some reason, the ghouls like to spread disease, degradation, and pain—it makes them feel powerful and special.

Below the subhumans—imps and digital-fractal ghouls; the hybrids that are part human, part animal; and the reptile worlds—is a place that all the ghouls degrade to eventually, over eons. It is utterly fascinating . . . it is a place of "no separation."

Let me explain. Each of the digital-fractal, semi-human ghouls is separate from all the others, so there is one to the left, another to the right, three up high, and six down low—there is space between them all. They seem to have individual thought processes and identities slightly different from each other. But when they degrade over thousands of years, they eventually lose their separate identities and become globbed together one to another; all the ghouls in that very low, degraded state seem as one.

That coagulated "oneness" or lack of separation looks like a brown lumpy wall. Here and there are bits of what the formerly individualized ghouls used to be, incoherent body parts and bits sticking out of the wall in a very eerie way. So you see a part of a sharp beak, the edge of a crown, and half a human eye protruding from the face of the wall.

Imagine a massive brown wall, miles long and very thick, and projected from its surface are bits of human bodies and things you recognize: an animal's ear, a special piece of jewelry, part of an ax used to chop people's heads off, three shackles and half a swastika, the Star of David, the right nipple of a religious statue, or a rotting finger covered in blood that's pointing at you . . . and so on. It is very strange to look at and very frightening, as the power of the wall is immense. I feel it serves as a foundation to all evil, a platform on which the higher ghouls stand.

The function and exact length and breadth of the wall eludes me, as I have only ever seen it eight times, so there's still much to learn about it. But it forms a great power, the power to crush and control humanity and the ability to carry humans to raving madness and extraordinary cruelty. This form of insidious maliciousness is endemic to all the ghouls. It is in their souls, just as evil is endemic to some humans in their silent hate, petty jealousies, or actions taken to cause hardship or difficulty to others.

For example, the Outer Matrix is made up of all those ghouls who seem to be outside of us, such as the UFOs, the Men in Black, and so on. In those worlds there is a ghoul-type that we call the Gollum because it's bony and naked and almost hairless, like Gollum/Sméagol from the *Lord of the Rings* films—except an inner-world Gollum when fully developed is about 20 to 25 percent smaller than the movie character.

The Gollums are born from a black pod that is very eerie: it's round and has stick-out appendages and gossamerlike wings. It's a fat, ball-like insect pod, but it also looks metallic . . . it's very strange. A pupa comes out of the black pod: it's like the body of a butterfly, but it's very deformed and distorted. Then from the pupa a baby Gollum is born covered in white slime that it uses later in life to choke people and/or as a control mechanism over its victims.

The Gollums' speciality is to attack humans, make them sick, and debilitate them and drive them to suicide. They attack gang-handed in twos or threes, although we've seen nine of them jump one person all at once.

They're very dangerous and hard to shift. They can make a human shudder and lurch and twitch with pulses of awful ferocity. They play mind games with people, taking them to despair.

The Men in Black are drones, but they're also very real and very deadly. They're linked to the black helicopters and the silent black planes, as well as the UFOs, Greys, and reptiles. They may be linked to the contrails— I have no proof of that, but we do know it to be true of the silent black planes.

And those genera of Outer Matrix beings, like the UFOs, are linked to the crop circle, as we have seen visions of crop circles with the Nazi insignia in them and other demonic symbols that suggest they're all part of the same game of enticement and entrapment. The core of a crop circle's heat is like that of a microwave oven, so that's how we know the devilish connection. The UFOs use the microwave towers of phone companies as a power source, so there seems to be a link.

Returning to the inner worlds of devils (the Inner Matrix), there is another dimension of the hell worlds that is above the imps and the digital-fractal ghouls: it is made up of humans still alive on Earth who exist in that hell world in their mirror-self state. Those "still alive" humans are degrading because of their dark sentiments and ugly habits, so they're already in hell in the Aluna mirror-world. You can see how bloated and demonic and abducted they already are. There are many types: criminal gang members; crooks; rent boys from gay toilets; porno kings; call girls; child abductors; serial killers; the criminally insane; gluttons; black magicians; and predatory humans who seem ordinary but are full of arrogance, silent hate, and disdain for animals and other humans.

If you have that secret disdain in you, you'll be drifting into the upper echelons of hell already. Most people don't know that. Your afterlife exists now. Also in those upper hell worlds are humans who appear only as a black silhouette. They have no features—I'm not sure why that is so. It may be people's darkness arriving in that hell as a shadow before the detailed human image of them does.

When humans die and find themselves in hell, their first reaction is one of horror and terror, as the other ghouls attack the newcomer fiercely, without pity, so it's very tormenting. But as time passes, the humans get used to the terror and become less scared, so the attacks begin to lessen.

In addition to the terror, newcomers are overcome with a putrid sense of disgust as to the nature of the hell they're in. The humans there aren't aware that the disgusting ambience that surrounds them is in fact a reflection of *them* and their disgusting lives. Platitudes and denials would have kept that truth from them while alive. So just as in life, they make excuses as to their revolting souls.

They pretend that the aversion they feel for their surroundings is justified, but gradually over time, the obscene nature of the dimension all around them becomes normal to them—they no longer react. It is like an open drain in developing countries: eventually you don't smell it anymore. So new arrivals also get used to the disgusting nature of things and eventually find it quite pleasing, since it reflects their inner sentiments (of which they're not usually aware).

Over time, humans in hell may begin to mimic the other ghouls and do as they do, promoting and projecting evil, as these were their natural tendencies in life. In this manner, humans start to lose their human form and degrade to become like the digital-fractal ghouls or the imps. They do so over time without ever noticing it, just as alcoholics might become podgy faced and blotchy and overweight without ever realizing how ugly they're becoming.

This is the hell of no return, for once people begin to degrade and lose their human form, they become digital-fractal ghouls, never to escape. They lose their limbs: the lower legs from the knee down seem to go first, then the upper legs, and finally the arms; and then the human becomes just an upper body with a grotesque face. Losing their limbs, they begin to lose mobility and hence, the ability of "separation" . . . which is the first part of the descent into the brown lumpy wall, a process that may take thousands of years.

Of course, some souls escape the hell worlds if they come to an act of contrition and go the other way. But I know very little about how those escapes come about. The beings just said that it's difficult and takes time, but it *is* possible.

Dogma sinks most people. Almost all dogma and spiritual information is designed to carry you toward the gates of hell, via elitism and grandeur and a feigned spiritual or social superiority. So the empire of the ghouls hides in wait, masquerading as religious and spiritual help.

A friend of mine was watching the hells one day, and she saw the corpse of a famous Indian guru on a slab in a mausoleum. As she approached the body, a most horrendous 12-foot-high ghoul, dark and dangerous, jumped from it. All the devotees bowing and scraping over the years had fed the being that hovered over the guru's corpse, making the ghoul very strong and large. Of course, the guru took himself to hell in the first place by pretending to be God. Posing as a divine human, allowing people to worship you, is an egocentric power trip that rots your soul and carries you to perdition.

There were 35,000 ghouls between us and the Camelot doorway. They knew eternity is on the other side of the door, so they stood there guarding it, hoping to be granted passage—which, of course, would never happen. Quite the reverse: all those 35,000 were finally killed and gotten rid of bit by bit.

While they were there, we couldn't have gotten to the Shimmering Door that stands at the gates of Camelot. As each ghoul collapses and gets rubbed out, the celestial light emerges one small dot at a time, ever so slowly—so slowly as to be imperceptible at first. If you were to put 35,000 little dots of light into the space of the darkness that you see when your eyes are closed, your "inner panorama" would become as bright as day. That's why celestial men and women can close their eyes and see a bright, heavenly light, for they're not inhibited and cut off by the darkness of their souls, so they're not surrounded by tens of thousands of ghouls blocking the light.

Most humans aren't bothered by their dark, nor are they really aware of it. They like their power trips and the accoutrements of modern life, designer stuff, and they don't think about how many fumes their cars belch out or how many animals they kill to stay fat and happy. Nor does hurting people or standing over them bother them as long as they get on with money-grubbing and feathering their ivory towers while preening their egos.

But a terrible thing has been occurring recently: the door of people's escape is closing; many humans don't have the time to process their dark before the end even if they wanted to.

Thinking about this and the students I teach, I found that the idea of the relentlessly closing door bothered me very greatly. I could see how many are rotting their souls or doing nothing very much and how some are even falling backward. Many will never get out of the hells they're already in, for the lower ones created by sentiments of materialism, greed, and silent hate are most trapping: they go very deep down into an endemic evil, people can't escape themselves, there's nowhere to run, and there's no system of pardon or rescue. You have to rescue yourself.

Then I realized that if I at least moved some people up a notch or two to a higher hell than the one they're in right now, it might help them enormously. So I've had to be happy with the hope of that marginal result rather than some better one or a complete escape, which most people (94 percent) will never manage.

It is jolly odd to walk around a shopping mall and realize that nine people out of ten are so imbued with their celebration of the dark and their cruel, egocentric fascination with self that they belong to the ghouls while alive, and that they're already in hell in the Aluna mirror-world. It's even odder to consider that they'll never get out or ever be any the wiser—before it's too late. They'll die in that state.

The technology of hell is most interesting; I've found it a hard but fascinating study. I seek to learn more. The two Sacred Beings I call "Purple and Blue" came to me, and they spoke to me for four hours. They gave me extraordinary and accurate details of the world today and the future of the children and the scattered Camelots. They asked me to go back to the hell worlds for another 28 Aya journeys—it's a Kali thing, anti-ghoul retribution. When I'm finish with those journeys, I'll eventually have my Ph.D. (piled higher and deeper, as they say) in the study of the ghouls.

I saw my ol' aunt Joan down there—she was very cruel. She looked very demented walking about with a strange lurch that looked very silly. Her face had collapsed on one side. I also saw Hitler, but I wasn't prepared to take him on. The Pope has many dirty habits—I've seen him there—he won't make it. And the queen of England has four bizarre entities inside her that have taken over.

I looked for Sai Baba, but I couldn't find him at first; then later I saw him hand in hand with a small child—it looked bloody suspicious. I trotted off to see if I could find Dick Cheney: no luck, but I did find Donald Rumsfeld—he's on the way out, too. I also saw Bush; he's not looking his best either, but he'll last for a bit. Next time I'm going to look for Mick Jagger, Nicole Kidman, and Jack Nicholson . . . should be fun.

Now when people say, "Go to hell, Stuie," I can say, "Certainly, who do you want me to look for?"

This is the most fun I've ever had. I fell in love with Kali—she is one of the most fantastic beings I've ever heard of. She's blue, like all the Hindu gods, and she has four arms. When she gets angry, it is very frightening. She scared me anyway.

SEX AND ANTI-GHOUL PROTECTION

17

Before we talk about protection, it might be a good idea to discuss the common threats, as most people never realize that they're in danger. I find the protection side of things to encompass some of the most interesting facets of the Aluna, but then again, protection and fighting the ghouls is kind of my speciality. I've been involved in hundreds of fights and missions and attacks on them. The ghouls are not keen on that Mr. Stuie Wilde bloke one bit! So protection has been vital for me.

Your biggest worry in life is the humans. This is because ghouls get inside the human body, where they stay warm, feed, and incubate. They're created out of people's evil, and some are incubated in metallic-looking pods that, as I mentioned, hang off people's ceilings, like the Gollum pods. Some have mothers like a queen bee that can give birth to a million ghouls a year. No one knows how many ghouls there are—billions, probably.

The etheric field of the human body has a slight influence up to nine feet—I've measured that. But it has a very powerful one inside of four feet. The ghouls jump. Within the four-foot range is dangerous, so crowded elevators are a no-no.

Remember that 94 percent of humans are gray: they have no color. They're like cardboard cutouts; their destiny has been removed from them—captured. The gray ones suck energy. Some are real predators—rapists, stockbrokers, crooked taxi drivers, whatever—but *all* gray humans suck energy, as they know their life force is ebbing. So avoidance is best, and close contact is terrible.

Love keeps you safe. It appears as vast and complex fractals that are often golden or rose-colored in your logo. But if there's *evil* in your logo, you're more vulnerable. If you have a lot of love for humanity, the golf balls of evil bump up against the edge of your crown chakra, and they proceed no further; then they start to travel back toward the person who created them. Often the golf balls hover in the middle distance, seemingly confused. I think they just wait for another victim to pass.

Women are vulnerable to ghoul infestation because sex involves penetration. When having sex with a reptile male human, it's normal for his ghouls to try to enter the belly/uterus of the woman. So sex with low-life men is a dangerous business that can lead to long-term digestion problems and difficulties with sexual organs, irregular and/or painful menstruation, and intestinal troubles.

When the ghouls lie *on* your belly rather than in it, which is common, they'll make you feel nauseated. If you experience that nausea, then use your hand as if it were a flat cooking instrument such as a spatula and run it down your stomach and prize them off, like scraping an omelette off a frying pan. This works.

The ghouls in your belly from sex with dubious men are harder to be rid of. Some shamans know how to get them out, but I devised a self-help method that also works. When a woman has an orgasm with no one else present, some of the ghouls follow the heat out; of course, they return a few minutes later. If the woman is lying down on a bed, say, the ghouls always come out to her right—never left—and they hover in the area between her ankles and her head. Most of them are located in the vicinity from the woman's thighs to her head, and they're never more than one and a half to two feet away from her body. And the highest they get off the bed is between 12 and 18 inches, not much higher.

The average hovering ghoul that comes out is about 12 to 15 inches high and 8 to 10 inches across. It is usually only the head and maybe part of the upper body that's hovering there. The rest of the ghoul just degraded over time, so it has no lower body or legs anymore. Ghouls look human, but deformed. Some have sharp teeth, and they spit a venomous pulse that's often lime green or yellow, like pus—it makes you sick.

When the ghouls come out immediately after the female orgasm, they will be about a foot off the bed to your right. Pass your hand thoroughly back and forth through that area—not at high speed, as that frightens them, just at a slow, deliberate speed. Do that, even if you can't see them to break them up. Blow a warm love in that direction, and that will usually fry them or degrade them so they can't get back in.

You may have to perform this ceremony a few times, as some women carry 40 ghouls in their midriff, kidneys, lower back, and reproductive areas; and because of the numbers, not all come out at once. Then maybe there are some very powerful ones in that region that only a shaman can get out.

It takes grace to remove the ghouls from a human forever so that they never come back, as the getting of grace makes the ghouls very sick and so they leave. You'll find that any medical symptoms in that lower area will improve as you perform this method. (Gay anal sex isn't my department, so I don't know how to fix that ghoul issue, except to suggest grace—sorry.)

Women sell themselves sexually to protectors, which is why so many pretty girls and supermodels who come under a lot of sexual pressure and attention have muscular goons as boyfriends—beauty and the beast. If you *have* given yourself away to a goon protector, then you're going to have to look at why you did that and why you sold yourself down the river. Then you'll have to decide if you're prepared to ditch the reptile goon or not.

Sometimes women sell themselves to providers, and that's a variation of the same act of selling yourself into slavery for money and lifestyle benefits. Eventually you have to be strong enough to escape or the man and his ghouls will capture your soul and never allow you to be free. You'll be chained for eternity. If you agreed to be a slave, you can't bitch if the ghouls try to keep you to your agreement. You have to be brave and fight and face your fear to unlock the chains.

The ghouls can talk to your mind and make you believe that it's your own thoughts you're listening to. So humans get abducted without their knowing it, led along. The whole house becomes infected. Sometimes the ghouls are linked to the closet-fascist male, as he is often in power over others as the head of the house. His sentiments offer the ghouls what they want: control. Sometimes they're just in his body, and sometimes they're around the house in various corners.

Of course, both females *and* males are abducted by the ghouls, which usually entice them through self-importance and glamour, in the case of women; or with the men, it is more often power lust, violence, hatred, pornography, sexual perversions, and all manner of secret and not-so-secret evil. Humans are way more evil than you may have realized.

There is a renewal ceremony that I sent to the women in my Redeemer's Club called "Gray Sperm, White Sperm," which is printed at the back of the book in the Appendix if you care to read it. Gray sperm comes from men who hated you, who used you as a sex object, or whom *you* silently hated. White sperm is healthy and normal. This is from spiritual men who loved you and respected both you and femininity in general.

Many women (and, I suppose, gay men) are depositories of gray sperm; it is toxic and causes disease. The level of etherically gray sperm in you will depend on your activity in the low-life department. The Renewal Ceremony I wrote out for the women is very powerful, and the feedback from the hundred or so who have performed it is very strong.

The process is very sacred, and it really works. That is partly so because it carries you home to another place, one of understanding your femininity and seeing it as sacred and precious . . . not just as a warm asset in the protector/provider department, or for bonking blokes around the back of the Dog and Duck just so you can feel needed or for a bit of fun—Saturday night's "slip and tackle," as they say. The love of God is all to do with a love and respect for the feminine spirit; any degradation is the antithesis of that love of God.

Tricks of the Trade

Remember that gray people suck energy on a massive scale. They can't help it; it's in their reptilian nature. The danger is that they can infest you with ghouls, as the ghouls can jump, and it's not just in the sex act. We're not sure how far one can jump, but we've seen it at 15 feet or so. So crowded bars and pubs are a danger to you, especially on a Friday night when the weekly cattle market vibe is strong and every swinging dick is in there hoping to get laid.

If you're having a drink outside in the pub garden, say, cover it with a coaster, as the ghouls drop lime-green etheric pellets in your glass—mostly they miss, but you can never be sure. I saw one hit my glass of Guinness. At the time I didn't know what it was, so I asked . . . and a few seconds later the face of an alien Grey with buggy eyes appeared on the froth at the top of the glass. That's how I first found out the lime-green trick.

- Never drink from a glass with liquid in it that has been standing on a counter or shelf uncovered or in the open air.

- Small ghouls with wings try to get into your mouth, and it's very hard to get them out, so always cover your mouth when you yawn.

- Ghouls go for dirt and blood, so ladies on their moon should stay as spotlessly clean as possible. Cover any blood wound with a Band-Aid or a bandage while it's still seeping or bleeding. And avoid tattoo parlors or any place where there is blood, like abattoirs.

- Men shouldn't wear beards or moustaches or have unshaved stubble. There are small etheric ghouls that are attracted to and live in men's facial hair. If you must wear a beard, keep it short and very clean, not long and shaggy. Never kiss a man with a beard unless you're desperate—tee-hee.

- Always cover wastepaper baskets and trash cans—this is very important. Remove trash from inside your home regularly and place it in bins that are covered or tie the trash bag nice and tight.

- Cover the TV screen with a cloth when not watching it. The ghouls walk into the room that way. Strange but true.

- Keep all air vents and air-conditioning grilles clean of dust and fluff, and if you can take the grille off and suck the dust from inside the pipe with a vacuum cleaner, all well and good. They serve as entry points.

- Remove clutter and keep things Zen.

- Never step over a drain in the street. There are ghouls in the slime of the sewer below.

- When having a bowel movement, use wet toilet paper (if possible) at the end, after initially using dry paper. Change your underwear at least once a day if you don't do so already.

- Wash your hands thoroughly with soap many times a day. The beings once asked a friend of mine to wash hers 47 times in a day. If you can't do that many, try for a half a dozen times.

- Avoid evil relatives and friends.

- Never hug people or kiss them unless they are very, very warm—not just pretending to be warm.

- Avoid crowds.

- Watch for demonic children—they are very dangerous, as you don't usually suspect them.

- Put three drops of lavender oil on your crown chakra, one on your Third Eye, one on your throat, and one on your heart. Do this twice a week, and put three drops with a prayer into your bathwater from time to time. Once in the bath, put your crown chakra underwater for 20 seconds and say a protection prayer. Remember the word *uturungu*. It calls the jaguar to protect you.

- Avoid UFO sites on the Internet and UFO books and magazines.

- Avoid Masonic temples unless you're a Mason.

- Avoid Tantra, as it calls in the sexual ghouls very powerfully. And avoid anything that involves sitting on the floor, like yoga. The ghouls come up from a dimension we call "240-down," and they try to penetrate our private parts. This is especially so for women—that's why they get allergies and serious medical problems from doing yoga. It's rather deadly for them. The elitism of this activity is a ghoul trick to sucker the unsuspecting. Avoid any sitting-on-the-bare-floor system of meditation or exercise. Use a mat instead; or better still, sit in a chair. If you must do yoga, always use a mat.

- Never go into Buckingham Palace, which is now open to tourists.

- Never go to Baltimore or Haiti unless you're very powerful and very experienced. These are big black-magic areas. Avoid New York if possible—deadly—and Jamaica is also hazardous.

- Never go to Israel (as I mentioned) unless you're Jewish; then it's okay.

- Pray to the magical animals for protection, but also send them love and pray for their evolution so you don't always come off pleading, whimpering like a crybaby.

- Buy a piece of black tourmaline and hang it around your neck or keep it in your pocket for protection.

- The shamans of South America put the leaves of the yarrow plant in their navels as extra protection, or they wear them in a pouch around their waist.

In conclusion, all low-life sex and perversions are dangerous, and low-life places are easy to figure out. If you pray to see, you will soon learn which humans are evil and which aren't. You have to learn to call the devil by its name and indict evil when you see it without making the evil person wrong.

So you might say to your partner, "I find your sexual traits unappealing; I'm leaving . . ." without going into how evil and depraved he or she really is. The less you criticize, the better, or the other person's evil might attack you. Just make your point unemotionally and leave. If you've dedicated yourself to the light, your inner guidance system will always show you the right way.

POISONOUS PEOPLE
AND DANGEROUS
PLACES 18

Here's an interesting tale. I went downtown with my kid and his mate to a rough area where he wanted to visit a used-furniture store. There were a lot of homeless and mentally disturbed people, drugs, and so on. I was there an hour. That night I lay down and I saw loads of etheric spiders coming for me. They had followed me home!

On another occasion I visited a shop that specialized in witchcraft. I was looking for an image for an article I was writing—they sold ghoul stuff: dragon T-shirts and such. An hour later I was surrounded by the ghouls, maybe 200; they were hovering in the Aluna inches from my nose, trying to spit and bite, firing dark waves of evil at me.

They made the spiders look very cheery in comparison. Again, I had been followed home. The ghouls follow the light, any light. You don't have to be a living Buddha for them to track you home. That night it took me four hours to get rid of them.

This has taught me to be careful. I can't go to athletic competitions anymore, which is jolly sad: the violence, racism, and hatred are too dangerous. A couple of days ago I sat in a restaurant with my back to another customer—he was a villain. I could feel that his emotions were ugly but powerful. His arrogance and revulsion for other humans felt like a black cloak made of rats scurrying about; the evil feeling hung close to me. He was very poisonous, and I became a bit sick. He got very edgy, and he came around to the table and offered me a plate of calamari. Strange, eh?

I have in the past watched someone pass me in the street and have spontaneously started to vomit. The first time it happened, it gave me a fright. Evil is much stronger than we initially realized.

There is a sweet woman I know who got very sick for other reasons. She had the standard cure, and her disease went into remission. Then she hitched up with a very cold, very dark man . . . she was lonely, I suppose. The disease came back; she won't make it while she lies with him every night—he'd be sucking her dry, and he'd have so many ghouls with him that she'd be their etheric banquet from midnight till dawn. I feel sad for her . . . she is so very sweet and so naïve. There is a drama to the karma of the charmer you select.

I was on an Aya journey once when I wound up hovering in a friend's bedroom. It was the dead of night. He was asleep on his back, and his wife was facedown next to him. It wasn't the world's most interesting adventure—I couldn't understand why I was there.

I asked to leave, and I heard: "Wait." The female woke up, and she slowly got up on her hands and knees, rocking back and forth rhythmically. She looked really intense and strange, like she was performing a dark ritual or a satanic rite. Minutes later she curved her back and transformed into a reptilian form that was similar to a large green lizard but with chunky scales, like armor.

I realized that the rocking back and forth was because she was having sex with another being under her that I couldn't see. It all felt very evil. She had an orgasm, and hundreds of rats came out of her private parts and scurried about the room. It was very frightening.

A few days later I saw a vision of my friend: he was in a hell world—he'd gone insane. I reckon lizard spit can make you quite mad. There is a hidden danger everywhere you forget to look.

I know a young lady from Baltimore in her early 20s. She's rather pretty when she togs herself up. She's into power and black-magic sex rituals. I wish I was allowed to post her photo here—you'd be so shocked; there is no way you would ever pick her out. She looks completely normal.

I met her boyfriend—he works for UPS. He is a charming guy: very gracious and soft-spoken and generous. If I told him what his lady was up to, he'd go white with fear or he'd think me quite mad. The only reason I know is that the beings took me in the Aluna to watch one of the black-magic ceremonies the girl performs in. Watching her cavorting and writhing and having sex and drinking the blood of dead children made my stomach turn. I was taken to see the ceremonies more than once.

Imagine chatting her up on the bus on the way to work in the morning. Your worst nightmare would be if she invited you home! This world is devious and secret.

The Pope has some disgusting habits. The beings took a mate of mine via the Aluna to watch him in his private chambers—nasty stuff. In the Vatican there's a ghoul that is 30 or 40 feet high—mostly red, yellow, and black, with long tentacles. It's like a dragon, really, but it looks more akin to an octopus blob. It is very graceful and imposing in a dreadful kind of way. It touches the faithful and tourists as they come past, infecting them. In Ecuador at the Aya ceremonies, I spoke to a lady who had seen the very same Vatican ghoul; she described it very accurately.

People pray in church to be raised up, but the ghouls have all the angles covered; "down" is the only direction on offer. Sometimes the ghouls try to jump in your mouth; it has happened to me several times. In the Vatican there is a statue of St. Peter. People kiss the foot of it in reverence, so the stone has been rubbed smooth over the centuries. Goodness knows how many ghouls have jumped into people's mouths off that one stone foot. Foot-and-mouth disease of your soul . . . free, courtesy of the Vatican. Callous stuff. We learn as we go. Never kiss anything's feet—animal, human, or stone.

Recently the beings have sent me via the Aluna into 25 or 30 different buildings, all of which are poisonous and deadly. I go in; look for the ghouls; and clean house, bucket and mop-style, like Mrs. Mop the cleaning lady with a scarf tied around her head, except *my* scarf is to protect my mouth from the jumpers and when the devils spit. I've been sent back to many of the buildings two and three times; one I've done six times. Some are private homes, some are hotels, and some are offices, but not many of those. I did an obscure hotel in Sardinia, another in London, one in Ireland, and one in British Columbia.

One hotel had 30 or more ghouls the first time I went, then 8 the second time, and one the third time, so it's an improving situation. The beings sent me to the cathedral in Wells, England, but I declined to enter, as it seemed so dangerous, so I did the lawns and gardens instead. But the next time on my journey I found myself in the cathedral spontaneously, without my volition, in front of the big stained-glass window. So there's no saying *no* as far as I can tell.

The ghouls are usually hovering on the ceiling, and sometimes they're drifting around at about shoulder height. I'm always very polite. I start by wishing them a good day, and then I ask them if they have ever heard of the Mancini brothers from New Jersey. They always seem a bit bemused, so I presume the answer is no.

I then explain that the Mancini brothers have put a hit on them and not to take it personally—business is business in the Mancini world. Then I rub the ghouls out slightly before they rub *me* out, and I leave. The Mancini boys are just mythological gangsters in my head. I mean no offense to anyone of that name.

Then after my work, I go back once the coast is clear, and I put St. Anthony's Latin prayer *"Ecce crucem Domini . . ."* on the floor across the threshold of the door into the property. I whisper the prayer one inch from the floor three times. That closes the joint and grants it the "seal of good housekeeping." (By the way, in case you're wondering . . . six quid [$12 U.S.] an hour, Tuesdays and Fridays; and I don't do ironing, and I don't do windows.)

Never go into a church, temple, or synagogue. New Thought churches such as Unity and the church of Science of Mind seem benign and kind to me, but the others can be very ghoul infested. It depends on the power trips involved.

Avoid the homes of evil people. Never eat their food. One bloke I know ate an avocado salad that a black magician gave him; it took the victim one year to recover—he almost died. One house I know of has eight Gollums in the driveway waiting for people to show up. And a bloke I'm acquainted with has an imp pod hanging off the ceiling in his sitting room. The pod is an extension of his soul. He would have to rub himself out to get rid of it.

Strangely, the imp pod is off-white in color, sort of "yellow pus" looking. It resembles a pupa, the cocoon an insect grows in. Most imp pods are black or gunmetal gray. They normally look like complicated microphones, eight to ten inches long, hanging from the ceiling.

Later I discovered that there is an etheric witchetty grub in the yellow pod on the bloke's ceiling, except the grub is enormous—several feet long. (Remember that the inside of the pod is bigger than the outside.) Strangely the slug that will secretly try to eat him is exactly like he is in life. He embezzles money from people without their knowing it, forging documents and so forth, so he's like a slug feeding off others secretly. Karma is so precise.

There is a famous vineyard in France that a mate of mine told me has a black-magic temple in the basement—she went and saw it. She said the lord and master performs rituals with virgins and blood to honor the arrival of the new wine. I'm not sure how you feel about the new Beaujolais, but I'm a bit skittish m'self!

Buildings retain an etheric memory about what happened there in the past. It's not just the presence of ghosts, but digital-transdimensional beings (ghouls) that reside there now because of a current evil or a past one. There is a battlefield in Virginia that is very eerie: you can see the soldiers lying dead. Some are hovering about listlessly 150 years later—mucky-moo.

Avoid urban alleys because the Dumpsters and men urinating there attract those ghouls that like dirt. All filth and clutter is dangerous; so are woodpiles. Don't stack logs against the house. There are entities that live in woodpiles that we believe are demonic. Stay away from noisy bars and hospitals; never go into a hospital unless you really are in extreme medical need. Obviously, avoid swingers clubs, S-and-M joints, gay toilets, bathhouses, strip clubs, and brothels. Try to stay out of trouble, and avoid people who smoke pot like they've got the plague. Be clever: try not to touch people in the street. If they do touch you, say "Love."

If a person passes you who seems very evil, quietly say "Uturungu," and make a slight splitting sound, as if you're sending/spitting the word *uturungu* over to the person passing you. The ghouls are scared of that word; it means "jaguar" in the Quechua language. They cower, so it stops them jumping at you.

Finally, try to only bonk people who have warmth and a soul, who aren't cold and cruel. Avoid those who pretend to love you, who make a show of being nice but are actually vindictive and evil. And remember that just because your spouse or lover hasn't eaten you in 30 years doesn't mean he or she isn't going to bite ya tits off tomorrow; sometimes the ghouls in people need time to incubate to become an extraordinary reptilian power.

Remember 94 percent of humans in the Western world are predators, freezing cold and full of disdain, so 94 percent spell *D-A-N-G-E-R*. They can spike your soul and poison you forever. You have to love them and not be scared of them, but then again, you have to offer a wide berth to those who are devious and nefarious. You do this in silence, without criticizing them or making them wrong.

The ghouls have a thousand and one different expressions and facial abnormalities, but what's fascinating is that I now see those same expressions and facial nuances on people in the street. It's very faint, but I can still see it, so I know ever more certainly who is possessed and who might be ghoul free. The ghoul-free kind are hard to find—you want to hug them and congratulate them and put them in a museum as rare specimens.

Make some prayer water. You take a bucket of pure water, like the distilled variety that's used in cars, and pray over it several times during the day, and you might put a crystal and white rose petals in it and leave it in the moonlight overnight. Then if it's sunny, leave it in the sun for two hours. Afterward, take the water and sprinkle it in every corner of every room in the house, saying a few words of protection or a sacred prayer. And having an enema with the same water works very well for you internally, as does a douche for ladies (when a woman is very evil or if she has an evil lover, the ghouls congregate in her private parts in droves, as I mentioned).

A woman appeared to me in the Aluna, a witch, asking me to help her rid herself of her devils. I know her in 3-D. She is so evil that I thought to refuse, but something told me not to. I felt a benevolence for her even though she's so very dark.

I didn't have a clue what to do, so I asked the Sacred Beings for advice. They said that I should ask her to stimulate herself to orgasm and that I should wait. I protested a bit, explaining that I was English and it wasn't my cup of tea hanging about in this kind of situation. But the beings were most insistent, so I agreed.

It didn't actually take very long, much less than five minutes—maybe because it was in the Aluna, not in real 3-D, so things move faster. When the lady released that sexual energy, 60 ghouls came out of her private parts, one after the next.

So I knocked that lot off and tried to leave, but the lady said that I had to wait for her to do it three more times. I told her I was rather busy and rather English and to call me in the Aluna when she was almost ready, which she did. Her second orgasm produced 30 ghouls, some of which came out of the other end! And her third try slipped a dozen more, and her last effort was good for half a dozen. It's a shame she couldn't ejaculate out of her black heart, as that would have thrown up a battalion or two from there. Still, I did what I could with what little I knew.

"Next! Doctor Stuie will see you now."

"Next" turned out to be a man who is very famous and very rich and very well connected; I think he's friends with the queen of England. He's one of the most disgusting people I have ever met: poisonous like a tablespoon of strychnine. Kali is after him—stalking him. But he is very hard to get to, as he is Jewish and very well protected. We're not allowed to tamper with the Jews in the Aluna. It's like taking on a dozen Mike Tysons.

The evil man has had a secret lover for 30 years—she is the wife of a well-known English lord. She showed up in the Aluna and asked me to run her a bath. (English nobs are very bossy, I should have mentioned.) I don't do baths, but it was too late. So I obliged.

Then after an hour or so, she lay on a bed in the room next door and performed a few rituals a bit like the other woman, and every time she had an orgasm, she spat at her evil lover. It was rather alarming. I wasn't expecting it. I got the impression that she resents him a bit, as he hasn't treated her well. He's got millions, but he's famous for being stingy. I think Kali sent her, since I would have never thought of that. . . . Anyway, I'm scanning for news of the bloke's downfall. I love Kali. She really is the big Mrs. Mop in the sky.

It's not hard to see who is evil and who is not; then again, the most evil man I know is very logical and reasonable, and he hides behind his Mr. Nice Guy routine. He is an incarnation of a very high-up Nazi and one of the cruelest of the Roman emperors. If you bumped into him, you would get conned, as he is a master of slick talking. But most people who are evil ooze charm, so you can't tell.

If you start to learn to understand people's eyes, what they're saying with them, then you'll see things others don't see. The reason I know so much about people is that I watched them in silence for decades, and when they made a strange grimace with their lips, I'd do the same—and soon I knew what each signal meant.

I see things that no one else can usually see; then I teach it to my students; and as soon as they've seen it at least once, they know what it is, what that subtle sentiment is called, and how hatred is so cleverly hidden. You have to want to know human secrets to study this stuff, and when you discover them, you won't be very impressed . . . but will become ever safer.

KALI THE DESTROYER 19

One of the most mysterious beings we have seen in the Aluna is the Goddess Kali. She is real and very powerful; she is both the creator and the destroyer. She is less than the Goddess of a Trillion Universes (her mother) but still very powerful. We have seen visions of fields of wheat that were black and dusty, and as she passed over them, they instantly sprang to life.

As I said, she was born from one of the 752 flowers that are part of the appendages of the Goddess of a Trillion Universes. She commands tens of thousands of worlds and dimensions that are huge, vast beyond comprehension. Our planet is just a speck of dust in a tiny solar system rotating in a galaxy that is smaller than one cell in Kali's little finger. You and I are microbes on that speck of dust. That is why I try to teach you to comprehend your irrelevance—it helps you.

Her world (what she *is*) oscillates at seven cycles a second. The pulse of the Shimmering Door is four cycles a second, and you can say that we humans oscillate at the rate of our heartbeat, so just over one pulse a second. It's impossible for a human to directly experience the Kali seven-cycle pulse for more than a few minutes, for it carries one away in a frightening way and makes one very queasy—we're not used to it.

One day in a deep meditation, I asked to see her, and I felt a tapping in my sternum: *donk, donk, donk* . . . I counted and realized there were seven taps. Then, seconds later, I felt the seven-cycle pulse start up; it seemed it was in my belly, rising toward my throat. In less than a few seconds, I was quite unwell. I asked for it to stop.

My friend Udita Chohan is one of the greatest visionaries I have ever met. She is pinpoint accurate in her perception of the dimensions. She has the celestial power like no other. It was she who told me how Kali came and showed her some of the worlds that the Goddess has under her guise. Udita could stand the donk, donk pulse a lot better than I could. Ms. U.C.'s power is greater than mine by a mile. She lasted quite a few minutes in Kali's intense worlds, compared to my few seconds. She said that Kali showed her a mystical world of sand dunes and parched deserts where the humanlike people ride a hybrid animal that is half horse, half camel.

Then she saw another world I mentioned: that of tall, humanlike people who live in very natural-looking houses constructed of stone and mud, where the occupants walk through the outside wall to enter. Kali also showed her a world where people have a vehicle to travel around in that is very high-tech, unusual, and complex compared to our clunky cars.

Essentially, Kali rules over many thousands of evolutions and dimensions of existence. Our human evolution here on this spinning rock is just one of tens of millions of places and dimensions where sentient beings exist, both physical and multidimensional ones.

Kali has a protective pod that she places around some people; it looks like a lotus flower made of gunmetal-gray segments like large petals. They remind me of surf-boards. It changes who you are.

When the force of the pod is strong, you become remote from humans, and their concerns are of no interest to you. It's not as if you wish them any harm or that you have any disdain; it's just that the Kali-pod takes you into another nonhuman world. You're in a different dimension even while walking down the street, say. You're not even remotely interested in anyone, and the yearning in you for the magical words and the mystical animals causes a great unfulfilled loneliness.

This is so because Kali is linked to the magical animals, such as the black unicorns and the white tiger, and those dimensions of great beauty call to a human's soul like a delicate tone-poem emitted from an exquisite celestial instrument. There is rapture in the beckoning of it. Udita Chohan told me that one remembers one's previous existences in those magical worlds as a yearning, an ache for *les temps perdus*.

I can only feel 13 percent of the Kali-pod that Ms. Udita talks about, but even that took me a while to get used to. It is a very otherworldly perception or point of view, as one looks at humans as a strange race, an alien life-form. You can see their ugliness and their horrible feelings as clear as day. They can't hide. It is most disturbing. It oozes from them like black sweat.

I frequently wonder why Kali hasn't rubbed us out already. So often I look at people and their demonic selves, and I can't work out what function they serve—like, *Why are they here?* I was taught that everything has to run its course.

Kali is here for the Renewal. She's the sacred cleaning lady in the sky, and we humans are probably microbes on a toilet seat. You have to warm up quickly and prove some worth if you're to avoid the celestial Lysol that's coming our way—tee-hee.

Kali is after the tyrants; so many of the top nobs in the world will fall within one year or so. They don't all die; some are arrested and others exposed. I saw one person in a vision: a high-up political person whom I knew Kali was after, as her people showed this to me in a vision—for some reason they wanted me to know about it. Three days later that person was dead, riddled with 25 bullets. If there is now a way of toppling the tyrants, that might help us all. What I love about Kali is that she doesn't muck about. I laugh when I think she might be part Sicilian.

Kali in the Hindu tradition is depicted naked. Her skin is deep blue, and sometimes she is portrayed as black. She is the one who strips away the illusion; it's said that it is into her black skin that the ego melts. She represents all that is organic and natural. She is often depicted with a severed head in her hand, as she devours demons.

She is one and the same person as the Lamb of God who comes to take away and remove the pain of the world, the memory of tragedies. (These higher beings can be many things at once.) The Lamb removes the pain-stain of the world, and Kali removes the dark entities and their human vassals. They are the same being in different forms. Kali has an alter ego, a human who was also born from one of the flowers, so in a way one could say that the Goddess is connected to a sister here on Earth.

It is all vast, so vast. Free your mind . . . then you'll see it.

GRACE AND THE HEALING WARMTH 20

Test this (never mind if you can't do it right away):

Close your eyes and get into a really deep medita-tion, and then when ready, start to think of love. Breathe it to people you know from deep inside the delicate side of your humanity, your pure soul, and sustain that for a few minutes.

If you're sensitive, you'll see wave after wave of rose-colored energy coming from a dimension that is 90 degrees to your right—they cross your line of sight right to left. You're watching grace flow toward you. It's there even if you can't see it.

In every wave that passes you, there is information—mind-boggling amounts of it, massive. In those waves is the entire history of every human who has ever lived in the past: who they were, what they did, when they died, whom they loved, whom they hated—all of it.

In the waves is the galactic topography and details of a trillion universes, and in it is also the sweet story of how one drop of water is making its way gradually from a Himalayan peak to the Indian Ocean.

In that wave is your story: do you succeed in the end against all odds, or do you fail? Of course, the answer to that isn't cast in stone until you die.

As an experiment, switch to sentiments of hatred and disdain and you'll notice the waves of energy from the right stop and come in from the left instead. The left-side waves are more black and gray; and they have a slightly harder, more defined edge to them than the right-side ones, whose leading edge is diffused.

This is a critical realization. When I discovered this, I decided to generate the hate waves and allow them to come in, and then I changed my mind to love to see what might happen.

As you flip your thoughts from hate to love, a triangle appears at the leading edge of the left-side hate waves, and it disturbs them: they hesitate for a split second, stuttering in the center of your vision, and then they retreat, stage left, from whence they came. Seconds later the right-side waves recommence—if you go to love, that is. This is the healing warmth . . . it can cure anything.

We know that there is a celestial dimension at 90 degrees to us. Some see it to the right, others to the left; sometimes men and women have sides switched in the Morph—that's normal. But whichever side you see the celestial is where the love waves originate, as opposed to the hate ones that come from the opposite side.

What is fascinating is that the waves are rolling in from one side or the other pretty much all of the time when you're in your feelings. They operate as an oscilloscope, showing you your inner sentiments as a waveform. You can see how coldness and hate make you sick—there are distinct adverse black-gray waves coming into your system—and why love heals for the same reason . . . ebb and flow.

The waves seem to slow down or stop completely when you're just daydreaming or thinking hard on a technical thing—problem solving, say. So that might explain why people who overthink for a living, who are obsessed with the glory of their minds, have little or no assistance coming in from the celestial. Maybe that also explains why they become gray and ghoulish and pasty looking—lack of God Force.

Let me explain. The human heart beats to the tune of its desires, and those desires are often discordant and contrary to the pulse of the Universe and the ebb and flow of the eternal Tao. That cuts you off and isolates you. That isolation is a *dis*-grace, a lack of grace. The punishment for cold feelings and isolation from humanity and the animals is rheumatism and arthritis and, of course, cancer, which is a cold disease.

Karma is perfectly precise; there are no innocent victims. So, you can see, you make choices every second of the day. Would you prefer the healing warmth and a chance for a long life, or will you get hung up on and titillated by dark things and die in the arms of ghouls?

There was a man who worked for me: he was the epitome of Mr. Nice Guy; everyone loved him, but secretly he was very dark. He embezzled money—did forgeries, false bank transfers, and the like. He and his wife stole lots of money. His embezzlement was interesting to watch, for it was certainly motivated by his greed and dishonesty, but the underlying trend was hatred. He knew that I helped people, and he wanted to do the same. But he couldn't do that job, as he didn't have the knowing, so he stole out of vengeance and jealousy.

In a hell world, I saw him being attacked by deformed human-looking beings we know quite well that have square shoulders and three claws. Those beings take one to insanity. Later I saw a vision of the same man floating in a river facedown—just a pale gray corpse in Prada jeans and a designer T-shirt, dead . . . another human failure.

I was sad for him. I loved him a lot, but I realized that it was his karma to die in the arms of the ghouls—not because of my 60 grand that went missing, but because of his hatred, jealousy, and vengeance.

Some of the etheric insects there are benign; and some are spiders, roaches, and centipedes. There is a strange white wormlike being that looks like an Australian witchetty grub. One of these etheric worm-beings jumped my friend in the chest and started to eat its way up to his brain. It took a while, but he was essentially a goner once it jumped him. It wasn't surprising that he's going to go stark raving mad; it causes the same symptoms as mad cow disease: one gets holes in one's brain.

Do you see the karma of being evil and cold? I could give 30 more examples of people I know who have collapsed one way or another—each was merciless and freezing. The End of Days is upon us, and with the arrival of the Morph, the forces of the Goddess are here to take back the earth. No question about it.

Now this isn't some kind of hellfire-and-brimstone fundamentalist rant that I offer; it is just to say the interlacing of the Morph and this 3-D world are facts—these transdimensional doors have opened, showing us that the Powers of Light are here. They can be with you or against you. They have no mercy for people who are cold and cruel.

One reason is that they can't really save individuals one by one; there is no time, and there are too many people. So they have to operate in clusters of people who are warm, where good results occur fairly effortlessly. But if you are all mind and intellect, you will be cold and distant—there will be a distinct glaze in your stare in the way your eyes look out. You will see humans as inferior to the glory of your mind and your ego's image of self, and you will see them as competitors or as danger, as they might interfere with your desire for self and its goals.

Essentially you will have taken yourself out of a warm evolution and placed yourself in a cold, hellish one, where you will attempt to make your mind into God. Obviously if your mind is "God," then you must be a divine being, one of great importance and specialness. The ghouls play on this desire for specialness, and they trap you, offering you nonsense and claridads and all manner of illusions so you never escape their clutches. This is because your inner soul, your logo, will reflect their sentiments, as the ghouls were humans who became ghouls for the very same elitist, cold reasons. They became what they are because they are like the cold person.

The danger lies in what is happening right now. With the arrival of the Powers of Light, the ghouls are dying and tyrants are falling and the devilish worlds are being brought down with every day that passes. So you're backing the losing side, and you will falter. Maybe not today, but sooner or later you bump into an evil that is superior to you—it will take you out, or a force of good does so. All evil finds a superior power up ahead. This is its destiny.

Udita Chohan and I and others are watching the ghouls die in droves—50,000 Gollums died in one night! As the ghouls perish in their millions, the humans they protect falter. If you are with them—or worse still, if they are with *you* in secret, in your belly, say—you have no chance; the victory of Gaia is shortly upon us.

Kali is the supreme warrior of Gaia. She is on the side of the animals and nature and is indifferent to the fate of human evil. This is a war that she is bound to win. And while Kali attacks the ghouls, the force of Gaia will attack human consumption and bring it to a close.

The End of Days rests in two distinct parts: the ghoul war and the human one. The battle against the ghouls is well under way. More than 100 million ghouls died in May of 2008—just in that month alone—and you can be sure the battle against the tyrannical humans among us will follow. A soft heart is your best chance.

THE BABY IN THE BOOK OF REVELATION 21

The Book of Revelation in the Bible is very important. It was dictated by a Sacred Being (the Gray-Haired Man) to John of Patmos in about A.D. 65. It is the story of the End of Days—you should read it if you haven't done so.

Some of the book describes a war with humans and the fall of the Great Whore, which is sometimes taken to mean the fall of greed, while other people think the Great Whore is the city of New York. What we only learned recently is that many of the events of the book took place in the Aluna, not here on Earth. We know that by watching it day by day as the situations of the story actually occur. The facts of the book are real and correct; it is not just fantasy and allegorical stories.

So, for example, in the book it talks of a woman who is human but also celestial. She has the sun at her head and the moon at her feet. She gives birth to a baby boy. The infant will rule the earth with a rod of iron, John of Patmos says. That baby wasn't born here on Earth. It was born in the Aluna worlds on February 17, 2008. The book says that a dragon attacks it, but an eagle comes to carry it away to safety.

We watched these events happen. The baby was taken to a cave in the Morph worlds and placed upon an eagle's nest that was made all of white eagle feathers, nothing else. Around that nest was another circle of white feathers, interlaced as a garland might be, to provide further protection. A woman who is part eagle, part human then stood guard.

The dragon attacked furiously, as it knew the birth of the Revelation's child marked its end. But the baby's protection grew rapidly to counteract the attacks. Indigenous tribes from the Amazon came around it to honor it, pray, and protect it. Then after a month or so, four people on white horses arrived to stand guard at the four corners around the child. Two were the Lord Shiva from the Hindu tradition and his wife, Kali; one was the Gray-Haired Man; and the final rider was a young warrior of about 20 whom I cannot name.

The battle for the baby's life raged for 60 days, but every day more and more protection came, and at the end of two months, the baby emerged from the cave riding on a horse's neck in front of its mother—who, as you might have guessed, is Kali. Its father is the Lord Shiva. The Revelation's child has four arms and is blue; like its mother and father, the boy is Hindu.

The child was surrounded by the other white horses and their riders, and it was greeted by a hundred thousand beings that were there to honor it. In the Aluna children grow very fast, so when the baby left the cave two Earth months later, it already knew how to ride and looked four years old. The baby is predicted to return in 1,260 days, in the fall of 2011.

The arrival of Hindu gods in the Revelation story might seem odd, but Christianity is a subset of

Hinduism—it's not a stand-alone religion. Krishna and Jesus are one and the same incarnations of the divine. So Jesus came from the family of the Hindu gods, from their trinities: Shiva, Vishnu, and Brahma; and the female trinity, Kali, Lakshmi, and Sarawasti. Essentially Jesus was a Hindu god, as was Gautama, known to us as Buddha. So Buddhism is another subset of the Hindu religion.

That is why Hinduism is the only religion that survives. It preexisted this age, for the Hindu gods have all done this Renewal thing before, 10,000 or 15,000 years ago—I don't know exactly when. Christianity, Buddhism, Judaism, and other religions are all modern creations. Only the Hindu gods have authority here on Earth, as this is their domain from way back in our prehistory, and they are in charge of this evolution. There must be other places humans exist, and the Hindu gods may not be in charge over those evolutions. I just don't know. But here they rule, as they created this age of civilization from 4000 B.C. to now.

The Revelation child that was born recently is well known in Hindu literature, which was written thousands of years before the Bible. It is the long-awaited tenth incarnation of Vishnu. The boy is known to the Hindus as the Lord Kalki. It was predicted that Kalki would come at the End of Days in the final yuga (age).

Vishnu is often pictured with a rod known as a mace, and that is precisely the child's rod of iron that John of Patmos spoke of, so he was correct. It can kill a hundred thousand ghouls with one swipe, and Kalki can turn a man to ash with one look. That is the power that has arrived to protect the Brave New World so humans can be given a new start. Our future as a species is assured.

After the birth of the child, the dragon tried to kill the mother. She has three simultaneous identities: she is Kali, she is the White Buffalo Calf Woman of the Lakota tradition, and she is the Lamb of God that came to remove the pain-stain of the world. But she is also a real female human doing ordinary things that all humans do, so that is her fourth identity. She, like many of us, can see in the Aluna, so she fought the battle against the dragon there while her physical body was here in 3-D. That battle took place mainly at night—it ensued for 58 days out of 60.

Now you have to remember that the mother is a real human who gave birth to the Aluna baby (Kalki) mentioned in the Book of Revelation. In the book it says that she has one foot on the water, the Morph, and one foot on land as a human. John of Patmos was correct. She eventually killed the dragon, wearing it down bit by bit, employing many methods to hurt it, including firing golden bullets at it from her fingers, but in the end she fatally injured it using a very innocuous item: a child's rubber ball.

The Gray-Haired Man that gave John of Patmos the Revelation story in the 1st century A.D. is also the magical child Kalki that is born 1,900 years later. He is a Hindu, as is the child. He is related at the god-level to the child's mother, Kali, and he is a real human man. The human who is the Gray-Haired Man from 1,900 years ago made a grenade, a very powerful bomb, using his power and that of two other Aluna fighters, and in it he put the essence of the datura flower, which is poisonous to evil. He converted a child's rubber ball into a deadly weapon that looked harmless so the dragon wasn't scared of it. The mother got very close to the dragon and threw it down the throat of the beast. The bomb exploded, setting the dragon alight, and it burned internally for seven days.

The dragon was the custodian of a very great and very ancient evil. Inside it were tens of millions of ghouls captured by the dragon that worked for it as slaves. In it were the Nazis, the emperor Caligula, and various black magicians who sacrificed children in the Middle Ages; and it was also linked to the devil worlds of Niburu, a rogue planet that is only peopled by Aluna denizens from the hell worlds. Those worlds are red, and the denizen of Niburu, some of which have incarnated here as humans, have a red eye when viewed via the Morph. The red eye is a sign of a demonic connection. NASA found the planet Niburu, and they calculated that it returns close to the Earth via its elliptical orbit in 2012.

In the hell worlds of Niburu are many vast cities and manufacturing plants that churn out drones, like the Greys and the strange Cobweb people that are covered in a sticky white web. Entire civilizations of evil began to fall as the dragon died. They looked to us like panels of a wall, like drywall, as the Americans call it; every 30 seconds or so a panel would collapse and fall over, a pulse would go out across the cities in the Niburu hells, and they would vaporize. This collapse of the hell worlds and those that were in or on Niburu lasted day and night for more than 40 days, after which the dragon finally died. One hundred million ghouls went to their deaths. The woman is brave; the greatest ghoul fighter ever.

As dragon was dying and the panels were collapsing, and as the pulse vaporized the cities of Niburu, I witnessed something else that was really extraordinary. I was in a hell world, fighting as usual, when I came upon the edge of a cliff. I couldn't see over it, as I wasn't prepared to get too close. One rule of Aluna fighting is never go into an area if you can't see the exit. The ghouls attack gang-handed, sometimes 200 or 300 at a time, so one needs the sight of the exit to stay safe. That's why I wouldn't go forward. The cliff seemed to mark the edge of a very deep hole—that's how it felt to me, very deep—and so I held back, wondering what to do next.

A being appeared as if in slow motion above the edge of the cliff. It was very black and very dark; and it had a triangular face, evil eyes, and strange black Mickey Mouse ears. It was the most malevolent being I have ever seen. I was very scared of it.

I fired ten times at my most ferocious, and I hit it right between the eyes and it didn't flinch. It didn't even blink. It had an ominous ". . . U talkin' to me?" look about it, as if it was pissed off by my silly efforts.

I knew I was in big trouble. It started to rise up farther above the edge of the cliff; then it leaned toward me very slowly in a kind of formal and deliberate way. I thought I was a goner. I have only once ever bumped into any devils or evil beings or monsters in the Aluna that didn't die more or less instantly—or after a fight anyway.

I asked, "Who's this?" Or maybe I said, "What's this?"

And a very calm voice from my right said, "It is the Beast from the Bottomless Pit." I could see the bottomless pit, and I didn't fancy it one jot. But the beast came up no farther from the deep hole, and a minute or so later it descended back down out of sight again in slow motion.

At the point when the beast appeared, the dragon had been dying for more than three weeks, and in Revelation it says that the Beast from the Bottomless Pit comes to make war on humans after the dragon dies. I don't think it's a war on innocent humans of a warm heart, but on the evil tyrants and the cruel humans in the West.

I realized that the beast is probably on our side, for if it goes around rubbing out evil humans, that will make the earth safer and cozier and more guaranteed for those who remain. So the beast is one more ghoul-removal device, albeit human ghouls, not Aluna ones. It's an ally, a supporter. Wow! Did that ever fry my noodle! When the beast comes out I don't know, but the dragon died in June 2008. The death of the dragon signaled the arrival of a great power here on Earth: the Solar Logos.

THE SOLAR LOGOS 22

Trevor Ravenscroft, the author of *The Spear of Destiny*, talked to me once for four hours about what he called the *Solar Logos*. He saw it as the return of a great spiritual power that he referred to as the "Light of Lights." The way he described it was as the return of the Christ consciousness made manifest here on Earth. In essence, he saw it as the coming to Earth of the Returned Jesus, but he also saw it as bigger than that, incorporating the light of the Universe and all the spiritual dimensions linked to man. He believed that the Solar Logos would transform the world into a form of heaven on earth, bringing humanity into a lush new era.

Ravenscroft was essentially correct, in my view. Lord Shiva and Kali, the parents of the Revelation's child, Kalki, are in the Aluna, as is the child. But they also incarnated here on Earth in secret in human bodies at the End of Days to be with their son, who is an Aluna identity, yes, but is also a human. In part, these gods came to establish the New Trinity, the correct one: father, mother, and son . . . rather than father, son, and Holy Ghost, which was a false concoction, a chauvinistic aberration that disallowed the divine mother.

Now before I explain the Solar Logos, here is a very intriguing fact: the Revelation's child has a sister who isn't mentioned in the book, a girl whose name is unknown to me. She would be another Hindu god, but I don't know which one. Aluna pregnancies last about three months, so the girl was born four months after Kalki—12:11 A.M. on June 26, 2008, to be precise. So there is a New Trinity of father, mother, daughter and the other trinity that includes Kalki, the son. I found it so beautiful that all was restored to a proper order with the birth of the little girl. She is blue and has four arms, as has her brother.

Legend said that at the End of Days gods would appear on Earth, and they would set the people free. That legend came about. The Hindu gods that make the New Trinity are real people on Earth, human incarnations of those gods, as I said. In essence, only the gods know how to fight the ghouls, so they were able to teach humans to fight and to liberate the earth, and so they came to restore humanity to the New World Order—which is not a political-military slaughterhouse, but an honor code that is laced into the Matrix. That code couldn't be placed in the Matrix until the ghouls were removed from it.

The humans who are Hindu gods know who they are, but they are very secretive, of course, since if it were found out and believed by people, then conflicts would ensue or worshippers would arrive and the battle would be all clogged up and lost. The American man who is the reincarnation of Lord Shiva merged his physical body over a five-day period with that of the man who is his son, Kalki; then a while later Kalki merged with his mother, who is Indian woman here on Earth, as well as Kali in the Aluna; and she then merged her physical body with her husband, Shiva, to make one Aluna being.

Let us call that being Trinity One (T1). T1 traveled to the moon, and over a five-day period, it merged with the Feminine Spirit of that celestial entity, and then it traveled on to the sun. The human gods could stand the heat because they are pure light, so the solar temperature didn't damage them. They felt it as pure love.

So in this way T1 merged with the sun, and it became a new enhanced being that we'll call T2, which is the Solar Logos. It is an entity that is three humans and the sun-moon combination, so five local elements make up the Solar Logos (man, woman, boy, moon, and sun), and then it returned to Earth. I'm sure the baby girl is in the Solar Logos, but she didn't travel to the moon and sun with the others. Her role is to help her mother, Kali . . . what that entails hasn't been shown to me.

Inside the Solar Logos is the Returned Jesus. But as Ravenscroft correctly stated, the Solar Logos is bigger than a Returned Jesus, as it is linked to the power of Krishna and all the Hindu gods. That's because at a higher level a celestial being may be more than one thing at once. So Shiva is Vishnu and Brahma at the same time, Kali is Saraswati and Lakshmi, and the human who is the child Kalki is linked to all his human incarnations, so that adds to him even more power. It is said the Solar Logos is equivalent to the power of a thousand million suns, the total spiritual light of those suns.

If you are a Christian, it might be hard to accept that your man J.C. isn't at the top of the tree, but that's because you may see him as only one being. If you understand him in a kinder and wider way, you'll see how Jesus couldn't have stayed just Jesus, the human from Nazareth; he had to return to the celestial heavens and become more in order to evolve, so he merged with the Hindu gods that were his original family. We don't know whom he referred to when he spoke of his "father in heaven," but whoever his father is, we know for certain that it's one of the males in the Hindu pantheon.

To provide a Returned Jesus on Earth is great light and great power, but it's not as large as the power of the Hindu gods or the Solar Logos, as it is a minor event on a small planet on the edge of an average-sized galaxy. So the Returned Jesus is a major event to us humans, as we would consider him God, but he is not *"The* God," and he's not even the biggest of the Hindu gods. But don't let that put you off, as the Returned Jesus will still be a fantastic celebration for all humans, Christians and others alike.

Any one of the members of the New Trinity of Shiva, Kali, and their son, Kalki, could have acted as the Returned Jesus on Earth, as the Returned Jesus is essentially three people merged as one being, but it goes further than that because the consciousness of Jesus is now so powerful that it can go into many people, and many different people alive today can become the Returned Jesus. They have to have the selflessness, humility, and vast love of Jesus, but they can do it. So the Returned Jesus that we'll eventually see on *The Oprah Winfrey Show* may be a woman, and then there may be five people, both men and women, on Oprah's couch; and they can all walk on water, levitate, heal the sick with one touch and even do many things the former Jesus of Nazareth could not do, as they will all have become what Jesus of Nazareth merged into when he passed on from the Earth plane and evolved to became more.

But it goes further than that. Jesus of Nazareth had a great power, so he could eventually evolve spiritually and merge with not only Kali but also Shiva and Kalki and many other gods in the Hindu pantheon and beyond the pantheon. That is because Jesus was a great celestial power, just as Shiva is a great celestial power, just as Buddha is a great celestial power. They are all from the same source, the same golden light, the same radiance. There is only the One Light. So Jesus is now a composite of many beings we consider gods, and he is linked to Krishna as well. He is a composite in a celestial hierarchy that we consider "The God." In the book of Revelation, the child born to the celestial woman is considered by John of Patmos to be Jesus. And John of Patmos, he was right—the child is Jesus, a third part of Jesus, as explained.

Of course, the Hindu gods are all former humans who lived on Earth many tens of thousands of years ago, and above them would be even higher gods, such as the Goddess of a Trillion Universes. She is bigger than Kali, who was born out of one of the flowers from the Goddess's body. So in the god business there is always one up ahead that is slightly bigger and more radiant than you. Where it all ends none of us will ever know, but it has been explained that it never really ends, as it is a loop like a Möbius strip, which goes 'round and 'round; and the highest of the gods just reincarnate at the start once more as a new person to travel through a trillion eons, to become eventually another godlike being, and so to create even more light.

193

THE HEALING
OF OLD CIRCLES

23

You can also finish this incarnation and close it out and start another life without having to die, but to do so, you must heal all the old circles and karmic loops you made with all the people you met. Each loop must be infused with grace and made whole, all transgressions forgiven, all evil shed so every association becomes pure in the end.

So you have to learn to forgive and allow all people who affected your life to proceed to whatever place they'll find themselves in; with your blessing and love, you send them on their way. You must genuinely desire nothing but the best for them, no niggling curses to follow them away.

Visualize a silver cord, make a small knot in it, place their names or a mental picture of their faces in the knot, and tie the cord and blow love on it. Then you set it on an imaginary hook to one side of you. This says that you're finished with them, all rancor made pristine in the light of your new wisdom . . . in light of your desire to let go and evolve past those people to better things.

If the influence or pain others caused you is strong, then you may have to tie the silver cord many times, and if you're not past them entirely in your feelings, that may also hold them to you. So you continue to let go of them, making the little silver knots as many times as needed to be free. The old patterns formed loops around you to bind your ankles because people don't like to let go and resolve things; the bitterness turns back on itself in an entrapping way. So you can visualize cutting the link and then making the knot. It is your wounds that hold you into this incarnation. Once you can release the wounds, the Brave New World opens for you.

After you have gotten rid of all the personal aggravation around you that held you prisoner, then you should let go of the political situations. The world is run by human devils—to expect justice is naïve. Tie knots on conspiracy theories and campaigns and the feeling of being put upon by the Fat Controllers; decide to leave no bones instead. Let go. Jesus said that if you realize his father is in every little thing, even a piece of wood, you do not have to taste death. That might work better than wondering if Eisenhower met the UFO Greys at Kirtland Air Force Base in the late '40s. Who cares if he did? The Greys are devils, and Eisenhower didn't win any awards for grace and pleasantness. Just a few days before I wrote this, one of our human Aluna fighters bumped into 5,000 Greys lined up as an army—not one survived; they all died. "Grey" seems to be going out of fashion nowadays. Tie the knot on Grey!

To evolve, you have to go past the troubles of society and realize that it is human karma to go through injustice for that which they caused others in the past, and you must be big enough to allow for it. You must move toward a pain-free zone in your heart, and while it can make you feel a bit lonely, it is the only way in the end or you'll perish.

THE RENEWAL 24

The reason the Morph descended and the gods reincarnated is to teach us how to fight and also to fight *for* us. It's all about what the Sacred Beings call the "Renewal." My knowledge of exactly what it entails is very incomplete. We know that it involves the descent of the Morph, which will asphyxiate the entire world population simultaneously on the same day. And we know that the Shimmering Door will appear in thousands of locations around the globe, to include every nationality, race, and color.

The children walk through the door into another dimension and survive the descent of the Morph, along with warm humans and minders who have practical skills. The animals don't die, as they can go into a trance called a *sull*—it's like hibernation; they use very little oxygen for the short time it might be required . . . say, 20 minutes or so.

That is where my comprehension peters out. I don't know when the children come back. Is it 20 minutes later, or do they stay in the otherworld (dimension) for several years, then return after the dead bodies on Earth decay and any potential diseases pass? What we do know is that they inherit a natural, organic world but one that is very rudimentary. No cars or oil . . . back to the horse and cart.

How many survive is a mystery, but, obviously, enough in each location to attain critical survival mass. What happens to the infrastructure of the world isn't known; maybe it's destroyed in a pole-shift. Also, the Morph makes the ground go to liquid, so it has no solidity anymore. Perhaps, then, the buildings fall into a deep hole, never to emerge. I've seen visions of that: the infrastructure just disappears, or it falls over and decays. However, it *is* known that some buildings will survive the Renewal, so whatever happens will not be entirely cataclysmic.

I'd never believed in cataclysms, but after thousands of visions and video clips that I and others have seen played in the mind's eye, I now believe in it all. It is a huge relief that Gaia gets her planet back, for I have a great love for her and her children; and for my part, I already know that *I* won't survive the Renewal, so that is my karma. I'm too old and unskilled in practical things to be of any use in the Brave New World. But I did fight for it, so that was my destiny.

Pray for the little children. Much love to you.

Bye for now,
S.W.

Appendix

THE ARRIVAL
OF THE MORPH

(Excerpted from *The Art of Redemption* by Stuart Wilde. Published by Hay House, 2007.)

In March 2001 I was in the town of Milton, in New South Wales, Australia. Fifteen people were at my house when something very strange happened. We were sitting in the front room where there are a number of daybeds (like those very large, wide couches and sofas you see in movies in large Indian homes). Suddenly, a very beautiful geometric pattern spontaneously appeared on one of the women's faces. It was circles and dots and triangles of many vibrant colors. They oscillated, moved, and shimmered across her face, spreading down her neck and covering her shoulders. It was both awesome and mysterious to watch.

There was no logical explanation for what was happening: No anomalous light effects in the room or sunlight from outside could cause the fractal, geometric forms that appeared on her skin. Further, the patterns were not static like a shadow might be; they undulated and sparkled and constantly changed positions. It was quite hot that afternoon, and one of the men had his

T-shirt off, soon realizing that he too had the same kind of patterns forming on his back. Gradually over a period of 15 minutes or so, everyone had them on their bodies to some extent. Each configuration was different—some had blue stars, others had little red hearts, and some even had leopard-skin patterns—but they were all a manner of images and shapes clear to see.

This was the first time we ever experienced what later became known as the *Morph*. It's a phenomenon, a transdimensional overlay, whereby a room changes its imprint or ambience in the construct of space and time, and the surrounding reality takes on a new form. It's as if the room exists in two states: normal and solid looking, and abnormal and not solid at the same time. The walls appear to go soapy looking, and the floor seems to become hazy and unclear, disappearing even though you know you're standing on it. Hazy striations begin to swirl in the air, floating together to form vortices and circles that you imagine you can travel down—doorways calling you to another world.

What we found, to our amazement, was that even our bodies seemed to go from solid to not solid at all. I know this may sound very strange, but others and I have seen the Morph thousands of times since that first episode in 2001. The experience on that day wasn't a one-time event or a group hallucination, and I ought to add here that we weren't on anything dodgy like hallucinogenics or drugs of any kind. Everyone was stone-cold sober on that curious afternoon when the Morph first appeared.

I believe that the Morph represents a new world, a supernatural dimension descending on our 3-D world. I find it to be the ultimate transcendental experience, completely changing our view of spirituality and extra-sensory perception. The Morph is for you and me and everyone. You don't have to be specially trained to see it. I'll explain how you'll get there in a later chapter, but first let me finish the Morph story.

What we found on that day as the patterns appeared on our skin was that our heads and faces became less and less solid looking, and we could see the detailed bone structure of a person's head or hands through their skin as if looking at an x-ray. People's faces then started to go hazy, and parts of them would vanish completely, morphing into another dimension. At times we found that we could see right through each other; bits of us were dropping out of our everyday reality and disappearing.

It wasn't scary, just very intriguing. But when you first see that the world we so believe in isn't really solid at all, it befuddles your brain a little bit. It took us a while to comprehend the process. Then one of the guys realized that he could put his finger into another person's head and push it through the bone of the forehead into their skull. As he did it, we saw his finger dissipate inside the person's forehead; and when he finally pulled it out a minute or so later, it was elongated and pointed and slightly wet looking. We laughed, and then gradually everyone had the courage to try it. Eventually we found that we could put our hands and arms right inside of another person's rib cage, and they could feel it tickling them. We played this Morph game for four hours, like children with a new toy.

A day later an upside-down Y appeared over a four-poster bed in one of the bedrooms in the house. When I put my hand up inside the crook of the Y, my hand and forearm just dematerialized. I couldn't see them anymore—all I had was a stump. So, I decided to stand on the bed within the Y to see what would happen next. When I did that, it got a bit scary, as there was a tremendous upward-tugging sensation coming from the Y-shaped vortex. I felt that it might suck me off the bed and take me someplace I wasn't ready to go.

At that moment, other people in the house came into the room, and two of the guys held on to my legs. It made me feel safer, but I didn't stay up there for more than a few minutes because I was worried that the tugging sensation would get even stronger. Then one of the . ladies took her turn to stand inside of the inverted Y, and we saw TV screens appear on her upper body, which were reflected on her clothes and skin as four-color images. Each was about one square foot, and pictures emerged on the screens, like video clips showing events regarding the destiny of the world. There were also images of galaxies and deep space and the outer universe. This lasted for about ten minutes when she also felt the tugging sensation pulling her up, so she came down off the bed. After a couple of hours, ten people had a turn standing in the upside-down Y, and each partially dematerialized. (Later in this book I'll show you how to create a miniversion of the Y vortex, and you'll put the tip of your finger inside and watch it stretch and partially dematerialize. Then you'll believe me, maybe . . . maybe not?)

Now let me move the story on quickly, for after those first two Morph events we found that it was everywhere all the time. When the Morph is very strong, you can see it even in bright daylight, but it's usually much easier to view in a darkened room. It often looks like dry rain with swirls and vortices in it. If you want to see it, you have to relax and learn to meditate if you don't already do so, for all the dimensions and experiences beyond this world call for the low brain-wave patterns of the meditative state. In essence, the Morph is the doorway of the Holy Grail—for me, for you, and for all of humanity. In the legend only two knights, Perceval and Galahad, got through, but now I believe that it's the destiny of thousands—if not tens of thousands—to make the journey. No one really knows why the Morph has appeared at this time. It's been said that it represents the descent of the Goddess, who is here to preside over a transformation that will take the world from violence and its yang harshness to the yin gentility of the feminine spirit. There's validity to this idea, in that the Morph is very soft; it seems to have benevolent healing qualities of rejuvenation and rebirth.

Another process that's developed out of the Morph is the concept of finding the Grail doorway, which involves redemption and deliverance. It's the logical final step of a long spiritual journey whereby you redeem yourself, not only of your transgressions, but also of the stored memories of pain that you acquired in this life. It's the reconciliation of a noble soul, by which you're made whole to become part of an eternal higher order. It's as if you step through the doorway going from a very solid yang world to a more hazy yin one, and you do that in order to immerse yourself into another evolution. It's not death—it's peering through the door and learning, coming back to adjust what you already know and then returning to look some more.

MORE ON THE
GHOULS AND
THEIR ORIGINS

I have felt that to understand the shadow process and the presence of the ghouls is a great privilege, for it is part of standing across a transdimensional threshold. Ten thousand years have passed and no one knew of these strange things, and billions have lived and died with no idea about the dark forces and how people were tricked and influenced by them. And while the ghouls sometimes give us fright, or they challenge us psychically, it is better in my view to know what's what than to be ignorant and blind and be a victim of them.

The study of the ghouls seems to have been one of the things I focused on over the last eight years, and now I know heaps more than ever before. To understand the origin of the ghouls, we would have to know the origins of the beings that are with the light, the celestial gods that act as our helpers at times. I would be enormously surprised if they weren't older than the Universe, so it could be that the ghouls are, too. In the macrocosm of light and dark, when talking about time frames longer than the life of the Universe, one can never know exactly what is right or not.

But in the microcosm of your subjective experiences, added to the experience of people like myself—and through what the Aya shamans have told us, what the tales posted on my old Internet site say, and your personal visions—we can in an anthropological way deduce things, working backward and watching and guessing what might have happened.

At the beginning of our Universe, there was a mixture of positively and negatively charged particles, and they collided at high speed for a long time and annihilated each other. If there had been an exact numerical balance of each fifty-fifty, there would be no universe, but there existed in the inherent mathematics of the Universe one more positive particle in every billion particles than negative. So periodically one positive particle found no other particle to annihilate it, so it survived. And the stars and galaxies . . . and us, trees, and so forth . . . are made up of the one-in-a-billion survivor particles. This is a positively charged Universe.

It could be that there is the same percentage of Light Beings as positive particles and that the dark forces are almost equal in power and number to them but not quite. The problem we face when speculating is that we know lots about the ghouls but very little about the celestial gods and spirit beings of the light. The ghouls are here on Earth, or close to it in the Aluna, and some are stuck in the astral . . . while the minigods and the Light of Lights are far away.

The Bible says that there was a fight between Michael the Archangel and Lucifer and his forces, and that the dark forces lost and fell to Earth. It is a simplistic explanation, but circumstances down here seem to back the idea that we are in a Luciferian domain, not a celestial one. Of course, we have no evidence that this was the result of a war in another dimension, but the devilish forces are a fact of life on Earth. It is way worse than people know, as the dark forces are clever at hiding.

We can see quite obviously that the evil of the human mind or the human sentiments, if you like, are the origin of many of the ghouls because many of them look like degraded humans, bony and malnourished, and they have dark thoughts and feelings akin to ours. But, then, in the hell worlds there are many drones and hybrids that look human, but they obviously *aren't* human.

Here is some information about a few of the dark beings that I have fought or that I know about.

The Gollums

The Gollums are short and thin and bony and about three feet tall. They are just bare skin—not much hair, no clothes or genitals. They have slightly oversized heads and buggy eyes and long, bony arms. Their skin color is a very sickly looking gray. I named them Gollums because they are almost exactly like Gollum from *The Lord of the Rings*. They are *not* good news. Luckily, they're rare.

They are precursors to ugly events. I was staying on the seventh floor of an apartment building near a bridge. At midnight I saw a vision of a Gollum down in the parking lot below, trying to get through a fence into an empty lot. I got up and penned the area with a powerful laser light that has a range of two miles or more. When I penned the fence, I got the impression that the Gollum had gotten away, as it had taken me time to get out of bed, find the light, and get to the kitchen window and shine the light across the street below me at the fence.

The bridge by the block of apartments is higher than the building I was in; it stands 130 or 140 feet off the road as it crosses an estuary. At 7:05 A.M. a man jumped from the steel bridge and landed below my kitchen window, not 20 yards from where I'd seen the Gollum just seven hours before. The man lay on the ground dead in a small pool of blood, with the finger and thumb of his left hand touching in the way some Asian people meditate. He looked very peaceful. I paid my respects and said a prayer.

He was 45 and dressed normally, not a street person or a drug addict. I wasn't sure if the Gollum had created the jumper in some way or if it had just shown up to witness the jump. It was very coincidental that the two were almost exactly at the same spot.

We do know that the Gollums make you depressed when they show up, and they try to take you to suicide. A man I know was attacked by six or seven, and they tormented him for a year—he nearly died. He was very dark, and the Gollums were incubated in his father's house . . . his father was a bit of a Nazi. It won't happen to you if you have a modicum of decency in you.

The Raccoon People

The raccoon people are just under normal human height, they wear human clothes and live in the forest, and they have very dark rings around their eyes, like heavy drinkers who have liver fatigue. I got a fright the first time I saw one. I was parked on a dirt road by a

stream next to a forest outside a Swiss village. *There*—
I looked to my right through the car window and a raccoon person had her nose against the glass. Eek!

These beings are humans who dropped out of the
reincarnation cycle and are now degraded, cold, and
evil. The raccoon people have a little lime-green ball
smaller than a tennis ball but bigger than a golf ball.
It is a form of etheric poison, and they drop them into
the mailboxes of people's houses. They may have other
tricks, but the green ball is the only one I know about.
The raccoon people are vindictive beings that lost their
grace and warmth.

If you get hit by the poison, you grow all hazy and
lose your balance, and you may find yourself having to
grab things to stop yourself from falling. A bewitchment
comes over you that makes you stare into the distance
as if possessed or in a trance. The technique to break
the spell is to constantly move your eyes about left and
right, and if a friend can keep you talking, it helps with
the same process. Warm baths do, too.

I have seen the bewitchment a few times . . . it is very
eerie. It makes you feel really sick and wobbly.

When it happened to a friend of mine, she went
deaf for a few minutes. I was talking to her from just a
few yards away. We were in a garden when the raccoon
people got her, and she couldn't hear me.

They try to induce you to go on the ground, since
they have a better chance to swamp you if you're down.
The lure to go to the ground is very strong and hard to
resist, as the raccoon people get in your mind and dominate it, confusing you.

I got hit in the same garden some days later. I got
into a bath with many drops of lavender; and I took a

bottle of vodka and spat the alcohol on my skin where I could reach by spitting, and elsewhere I just rubbed it on. Then I said prayers on my skin for a long time and lit incense, and eventually the bewitchment subsided. We learned the alcohol trick from the shamans.

The raccoon people are nasty. They promote despair, and they seek to abduct humans. They worship and serve a blob-type being that's 60 feet tall and red and black, with tentacles like an octopus. The Blob, as we know it, has a range of evil that spreads a hundred miles in all directions.

We fought one once, and once only. It was so powerful that five knights came from the Aluna into 3-D here to help us—we couldn't manage. The Blob took five days to die. It was in a garden of a pub near Stratford-upon-Avon, England, the home of Shakespeare.

The biggest of these octopus blobs is in the Vatican. It is also very tall: it reaches from the altar, where its underside hovers about ten feet off the ground, right up into the dome, and its tentacles go almost all the way back to the front door of the cathedral. When it dies, the Pope will fall—my guess is, he'll be exposed on perverted sexual issues.

The Parka People

There are small entities that live around woodpiles that I call the Parka People. They are about three and a half feet tall, and they look like they have jackets on with hoods . . . hence, the Parka People. They always move in groups of eight to ten, and they have child-like airs, so I reckon they're evil children who never got out of here. They don't seem to cause real harm, but we learned to stay away from large woodpiles or logs that are stacked for shipment.

The Nutters

The Nutters were discussed in these pages before. They are humans in the Aluna who were/are not right in their minds. When I was in the Aya temple in Brazil, I saw about half a dozen of them. They look almost normal except there is insanity in their eyes. They need to belong, and they come around hoping to be useful or to learn something.

In Brazil, I saw one of the Nutters trying to make herself useful cleaning the Aya temple by rubbing the wall with a brick. Mad! She was a very large woman with a ghastly floral dress on that hung straight down from her armpits. Her face was slightly deformed, and she had the stupidest supercilious grin that said: *See how useful I am!*

Another Nutter appeared in the garden around the Aya fire pit all dressed in cricket whites, with bat, pad, and cap. He was slightly bent over a coconut as if to hit it and score runs. He also had somewhat deformed features. And there was a young man with bony features and long hippie hair just standing motionless, gazing in the distance; and a young woman came through the place moving quickly—she looked like one of the New Age rainbow people. She had a big bag with plastic flowers stuck on it, but her eyes were completely mad.

Insanity forms a massive dimension of itself. I was once taken by the Sacred Beings for eight hours into the worlds of dementia and the insane so that I could learn about it. And while most of the entities are possessed humans or people alive who are stressed-out, who move around in their alter-ego mirror-self form, there are also many in that crazy Aluna world that would be labeled criminally insane here. The dimensions also include human beings who have been mistreated. There are children in there who have very large pumpkin heads; they are very loving but very damaged as well.

Listlessness, laziness, and apathy are mild forms of insanity, much like the bony boy staring into the distance. Fascism and control are also a type of insanity, as is vengeance and hatred of any kind. In those mad worlds, you see Nazi officers prancing about goose-stepping, barking orders at people who aren't listening, or there are men in dark coats who look like the character Mephistopheles.

Some of the insane are in dimensions of their own, but some are down here on Earth playing cricket with a coconut! The Nutters all seem to show symptoms of a repetitive, compulsive disorder.

The Mephisto

Originally the Mephisto (short for Mephistopheles) was the devil or demon that came from the Faustian legend in literature. You also see him in the Aluna as a male in a black coat. He is often very tall, anywhere from 8 to 40 feet high; he's very evil and very tricky. He'll play to your lust for power if you're prepared to sell your soul and fall for it. The Mephisto beings are very closely linked to cruelty and black magic.

I was asked by Udita Chohan to go to the west of France to a garden where seven children were buried. They had been murdered as a human sacrifice by evil priests a hundred years ago. Their souls were trapped, and their bodies were under a large boulder near the church. Guarding the place was a black snake with a huge head the size of a horse's. Next to that was a Mephisto—that's why we came to think that they're linked to child abuse and black magic. Udita paralyzed the snake, and I held the Mephisto. A bridge of flowers then appeared, and the spirits of the children walked out after about 15 minutes. They crossed over to another world.

The Astral Entities

The astral entities are humans on Earth in spirit form who never made it out of here after death. At the very cold and damp end of the spectrum are ghosts that haunt old houses that believe they're still alive.

In an old hotel in Ireland I watched as a female phantom dressed in Victorian clothes passed through a cupboard and then through the wall out into the hallway. She would have been in the building a hundred years or more.

Then there was a very emaciated chap I once saw wearing striped prison clothing like those worn by the Jews in Auschwitz. He was walking along the sidewalk at Battery Park in New York. He would have gotten there from Germany or Poland (where he probably died) because of his emotional link to a relative or friend who lived in New York or by following Auschwitz survivors over to America.

He was very scary looking because he was so trapped in his Jewish-prisoner identity. He liked it. He felt proud of it, and that's why he wore the prison clothes. He walked right through a group of tourists on the sidewalk as if they weren't there.

My ol' teacher said that when there is a cataclysm—like, say, the Renewal—and all the humans are wiped out and the world is returned back to a natural state, all the astral entities, ghosts, and demonic attachments are washed away into the dark spirit worlds and the earth is left clean. Eventually the man in Battery Park will probably degrade even further and become a Gollum type, carrying vengeance against humanity for the crime committed against him.

The Living Dead

The Living Dead are close to us . . . they are demonic humans in the Aluna. They often wander about in cemeteries. They are often very thin and emaciated, and they have hollow eyes or just sockets and no eyes. They are spooky to look at; sometimes they appear as walking skeletons—just bones, no flesh or clothes at all. They can attack, and we once killed a battalion of 500 to 800 of them. They came in support of a devil-god called Baphomet.

Baphomet

Baphomet is the devil-man-woman-goat hybrid that Aleister Crowley worshipped. It has an almost human face that is triangular, and hornlike appendages on its head that are in effect fractal tubes. The body is like a goat's except it has human-female breasts.

The Baphomet commands a strange energy we call the *hollows*. It is a form of bewitchment in which you feel very blank; life is not worth living, and you can look at a loved one and not care for them one jot. Nothing means anything when the hollows come over you.

Baphomet is bloody nasty, and at the time of writing, he/she/it is still alive in the Aluna. It is also linked to the blob-type beings. We fought with it on and off for two months, but we never killed it. We didn't win them all. . . .

The Black Imps

There are Black Imps that look like the Gollums, but they're taller—four to five feet—and more elegant, faster, and more agile. The Gollums don't move very quickly. We know that the imps incubate in pods that resemble large black avocados that have hairy skins. They hang down from the ceiling in people's homes on what looks like a piece of string. The imps are very much larger than the pods they're incubated in. There can be a dozen imp pods in one house in various rooms. The imps control various devil worlds; and they're connected to pornography and the dark side of the Internet, black magic, and blood rituals.

We know little about how the imps move or what their range is, but we do know that they're here "on the ground," so to speak, and in the devil dimensions. They are incubated from the need to control, especially when

GRACE, GAIA, AND THE END OF DAYS

that controlling urge becomes obsessive and demonic, so
. . . sexual domination, the threat of physical violence,
emotional manipulation, financial greed, and so forth.
In part the imps are fueled by a power lust—the lust to
own, control, and destroy. I've never fought any, so I
don't know how they die.

The Jinn

The Jinn are particular to the Middle East, especially
Egypt. They are beings of a human appearance that are
pulled in and sustained by a magician for his or her
dark purposes, like the story of Aladdin and his lamp.
They are usually concocted or called in via incantations,
the use of old Egyptian magic, and ritualistic masturba-
tion and the power of homosexual sex acts. If men and
women make love and have an orgasm, the energy travels to a higher use; but with men copulating, the energy
is trapped and hangs around, unless there is much love
and respect. Magicians in the Middle East knew of this
trapped energy and how it could be claimed and used to
sustain their creations, such as the Jinn. The magicians
that conjure the Jinn use young boys.

Much of the power of the Catholic Church is sustained by the same homosexual source and by the use
of black magic. It is harnessed to advance the church's
agenda of control and abuse and a callous disdain for
followers and parishioners. They are in the same Jinn
world, but using slightly different forces.

Insiders say that the power of the church is enforced
by a man we know only as the Green Cardinal. He holds
Black Masses under the church when special events are

taking place upstairs. I have only seen him in the Aluna once, several years ago. I was scared of him, although I stood my ground. He stared at me for about 45 minutes and never blinked, so I stared back and gave him the middle finger and a few kind words in Italian like: "F'you and your little dog, too."

I didn't have the power to take him on, but that was then—I am 500 times more knowledgeable now, which might also explain why he hasn't been back!

Some say that the Jinn are connected to the spirits of the dead, and that may well be so; or the Jinn are essentially the spirits of those humans who are in twilight worlds, like the Living Dead, or who are demonically possessed, gray, and evil . . . yet still alive, pretending to be normal.

The area around the pyramids at Giza is the world's capital for earthbound spirits. The Pharaohs and their empires were extremely evil. They were cruel slavers and black magicians, and they performed blood ceremonies and human sacrifice. The mummification of human bodies came from their desire for immortality—which, you may already know, is a ghoul trait.

The power of Egyptian magic and the Jinn is immense even today, and there are many entities that are Jinn-like and often dress in leather and fur and look like Mongol warriors, which is where all magic came from originally. They are summoned through warped sexuality and the desire to control or own others sexually and/or to use them as slaves. The warrior-Jinn types are very hard to shift, and they usually come in threes. They are attracted to rape and sodomy where one partner isn't willing—homosexual rape.

219

The China Tong

In 3-D the Tong are Chinese criminal gangs that abduct women to work in brothels using mind control and fear. In the Aluna there are also China Tong gangs that use bewitchment and the mind-wipe technique to capture women so they will lose their sanity and die and become their sex slaves in the otherworld. The abduction techniques they use usually only work on females who have been sexually abused, as those women are used to it, so they tend to go along with it.

In the Aluna, the China Tong are human in shape. They wear black silk, with two gold stripes on them. The biggest fight I ever encountered was to rescue a woman who had been gotten at by them. It took two months to get her free from the Tong—she came to within three hours of death. We got her out in the end and defeated the Aluna version of the China Tong.

Caribbean magic voodoo came from Africa. It is very Tong-like in that the rituals use blood and call in the astral beings, and so it puts the human in a trance-like state, open to temporary or long-term demonic possession.

There are many forms of African magic, such as juju in West Africa, and they would all have their roots in the Egyptian rituals and the conjuring of astral helpers such as the Jinn. South African magic uses the mutilation and sacrificial deaths of children, so it is even nastier than the rest—none of which is very nice at all.

Your protection against these conjured forces is to stay away from the people who conjure them and the places and ceremonies where they might be invoked. Trevor Ravenscroft told me that Hitler had a spirit medium who would emit ectoplasm from her vagina and Jinn-style beings would be birthed in the room. Obviously, if you're at a séance and a lady is firing stuff out of her private parts, you'll know that it's time to head to the pub instead.

The Dwarfs

The Dwarfs are very strange: They are short and appear wearing jerkins and baggy pants like they might in fairy stories. They walk very fast; they always look extremely busy. They're connected to the woods, of course, but I'm not sure how bad they really are. I've never had a problem, but like all transdimensional beings, one doesn't want to call them in, as there is much we don't know of them or their power. But they must be degraded humans going backward in their evolution, as they are stunted, very stocky, and short. They are highly rare to see.

The Greys and UFOs

I'll not talk much about these beings, as I have written about them a lot on the Internet pages. The Greys are like the imps that are incubated in a pod except the pod of the Greys is the UFO, which is a being in itself that can shape-shift and move very fast.

The inside of the UFO is very big compared to the outside; it is inverted in size like the imp pod. It can enter the 90-degree world, so that's why one can seem to blip out of the sky suddenly. The UFOs are sometimes the classic saucer shape; or they can be brown blobs, flying sticks, barrels that look like flying oil drums, or large triangles.

The UFOs are time dated, as they mimic whatever the latest human technology is, so in Victorian times they appeared as hot-air balloons and later, in the 1930s, as dirigibles. Then saucers appeared after the Germans experimented with aircraft of that shape in the 1940s, and after that the UFOs began to mimic the stealth bomber and became triangular in shape and dark in color. So the shape-shifting look of them has progressed through the ages. This tells you that they aren't alien spacecraft from other galaxies—just phonies.

And if they try to sell you on the idea that you have been chosen to deliver an important message for humanity, give them the middle-finger salute. The trick to getting rid of these pests is to stand your ground, ridicule them, and breathe love on them all at the same time; and don't give them an iota of fear to latch on to. Eventually they quit and go find someone else to harass.

The Greys are cowards—they are scared of light. They use sleep paralysis to hold you down. If they do that, put all your concentration on moving your little finger, then another finger, then your hand and arm . . . and you're soon out. Stand quickly and rush them— they'll flee. They are cowards; they don't fight.

The Reptiles

The masters of the Grey are the reptilians, and they're like dinosaurs or dragons, and very nasty. How they arrived at a consciousness that can influence the world as they do is beyond my ken. They attempt to possess the human mind, feeding on people's cruelty, and they attempt to live life through human bodies.

The shape-shifting reptilian human is real. The reptiles are old, so maybe they got their power over eons. Some say they come from the remains of the human reptilian brain—I don't know if that's correct or not.

The power of the reptilians is political-military. They are inside the minds of powerful humans who own and control the world.

David Icke has made a study of the reptile humans in the political world, and his assertion that humans can shape-shift into their reptile form is correct. I have only seen it twice, and both times it was a married female in her mid-40s, but that isn't to say that men don't do the same, just that I haven't seen it. I do know many others who have witnessed the human reptiles shape-shift, so we believe it to be real.

In the Aluna worlds, the reptiles are very strong, and they are very deep down: the deeper down a being is situated in the hell worlds, the more power of evil they command. Some look like dragons, 15 or 20 feet high, some are more like 5-foot lizards, and some are crocodile shaped; and there are some like large rodents with long snouts. There are flying reptiles that have wings that attack in groups of 30 or so.

All of the reptiles are hard to kill, as they are very strong and leathery, but their mouths are always open, so if you go in fast with your finger and make a turn upward into their brain, they die eventually. However, you have to be resolute in order to kill them, as you must get very close. I've done 500 or 600. The biggest was the Revelation-dragon reptile—it took three months of heavy fighting before it died. I was involved in the fight, but I didn't make the kill. The mother of the Revelation child commands a great power; she took that job and the honor of it . . . she greatly deserves it.

The Monsters and Hybrids

In the very deep hell worlds where the dragons and reptiles reside are many hybrid beings that are so ugly that one can't really describe them: beings that are part human but grotesquely misshapen, monsters with two heads and an eye in their foreheads. Some are part bird, part animal. Most are so bizarre that there are no creatures on Earth with which to compare them. Some beings are like structures: they are often cubes or circles that have a face in the center, or they are made of appendages or blocks put together to make a creature of great brutality and ugliness.

They have body armor and spikes on their bodies, and often they have large plates of what looks like metal to protect them. They resemble a black armored car, like a military vehicle with a face in the middle of it. They all have hate in their eyes, which are usually red in color. Some look like massively large spiders—say, 30 feet or more across—and there are black beetles that are the size of a small house.

They are all creatures that got lost on the way and turned to evil. Any being that is low down in the hell worlds is hard to get to and kill, and the monsters take a lot of effort to fight. They don't go down easily, as they're very strong.

The Fractal Devils and Evil Ones

The Fractal Devils must have been humans at some point, for they almost always have a face in the center of their fractal form. They are common. I've seen maybe 40,000 of these or more. They look like a rudimentary human face surrounded by a digital-fractal headdress and/or a partial mask. Some have teeth and drip blood, and some are more benign.

The older the Fractal Devils are, the less mobility they have. They can move back and forth toward you and away from you on a curved trajectory, but they have difficulty moving sharply left and right to take "avoiding" action. This inability to quickly shift sideways always proves fatal for them. They fire pulses of evil, but usually they miss or one's protection blocks it. Speed is everything in those worlds, and we humans are much faster than the Fractal Devils.

The Fractal Devils jump into people, residing in the area between the navel and the pubic bone in women, and the upper-chest area of the sternum in men. Shamans can get them out. I mentioned how women can remove them in the chapter about sex and the ghouls. Men can get them out if they go toward the feminine and softness.

The Succubi and Incubi

The Succubi and Incubi are stunted dwarflike characters that feed off people sexually, usually at night. They look exactly like the being in the painting by Fuseli called *The Nightmare*. I found it on Google if you want to look it up.

They are called in by sexual fantasy, sadomasochism, and extreme sexual practices. I've only ever seen a few of them. They are usually seen sitting at a sleeper's knees, just like in the painting. They're hard to kill—I've never managed it. We don't know how to force them out, but if you take to celibacy for a while, they do drift away eventually.

The Etheric Insects

The Etheric Insects feed off our energy at night, but we don't know what to do to get rid of them. I've seen maybe 20 different types or more. There are large black spiders the size of your outstretched fingers and smaller ones the size of a golf ball; then there are red ones and multicolored ones. There is also a form of flea that looks about the size of a cockroach, but it flies vertically rather than the way roaches move laterally, running across the ground in their horizontal position. The etheric fleas hover near people's legs, and there are midgets that swarm around our bodies, usually at head height, that are attracted to the heat.

There is nothing we can do about the Etheric Insects except become more pure, so we have to suffer them for now. As I said, they seem to get worse if you've been in a rough area of a city, as the energy of the street people there follows you home, and the insects come with it and hover around you.

Inner Matrix Evil

The Inner Matrix, as you already know, is a band of energy close to the Earth plane that contains the collective subconscious of humankind, those alive and all those who are already dead. When you lie down to meditate, you'll see the Inner Matrix as faces that flash in front of you very quickly. That's why I called that band of energy the "flashy-faces."

Sadly, it's usually all pure evil and hatred. Where the good part of the human mind is, is a mystery to us. We believe that it moves away to a higher world, and what is left behind is in the Inner Matrix, which is all the collective evil of our humanity. Also in there are some human entities that aren't totally evil but are just stuck, hanging about confused.

The Inner Matrix is all the souls of human ghouls that are trapped close to you. They play to your weaknesses and challenge your integrity and resolve, and all you can do is breathe love on them and endure them. You must never let them get you down, for they will try to take you to a madness that is the same as theirs.

Usually the human ghouls of the Inner Matrix speak to you mentally using sentences of four- or typically five-word bursts. If you remember former British prime minister Tony Blair's speeches, they were all delivered in the Matrix five-word, staccato style. This is evidence of mental abduction from dark forces within.

Eventually you'll find that the influence of the Inner Matrix wanes, but to do that, you have to process your shadow, as the ghouls use that darkness within you to connect to you on an energy level.

The Degraded Humanlike Ghouls

Aside from the Fractal Devils, which are usually just a distorted human face and shoulders with silly appendages, there are also humanlike ghouls in the Aluna that have entire bodies, like the Tong, and they move a lot more quickly than the other types. There are hundreds of species of the humanlike ghouls, so I can't go through them all here or the world would end before we finished. I'll run through a couple.

The Albinos are white human-looking beings with buggy eyes. They are very scary, and we have only ever seen a few hundred of them as a group. They all died, so we never had a chance to strike up a relationship or discover much about them, except the buggy eyes say that they're from a dark and dangerous world like that of the Greys.

The Cobweb people are bony and very strong. They are each linked by cobwebs and are covered in them; they use the cobwebs to suffocate humans. We don't know if we're able to kill them, as the one and only time they appeared as part of the battle forces of the Revelation dragon, a knight came out of the Aluna. He was very incandescent and honorable, and he killed them by attacking with his sword, moving it through the air at a blistering speed that is impossible for us humans to replicate.

The Clunkers

The Clunkers are another group. They are all about eight feet tall and are human looking, but they're constructed of metal parts that have bolts in the joints and elbows. They lurch as they walk, hence the name I gave them. They're not very fast. The Clunkers have a range of evil that we estimate is 30 miles. That range is somewhat predicated on how many are gathered together.

I was sent to a garden in France near Marseille with another fighter to clear the place of evil. Between the Clunkers was a gray mist. I wasn't sure if that indicated the presence of other beings, like allies, or if the mist was an appendage of the Clunkers.

I fought in hand-to-hand combat for four nights, one hour before dawn. My partner in the attack made a special purple arch in the garden to lure the Clunkers, calling to them to come over. When they got to within 10 or 12 feet of the arch, it zapped them and they died instantly. Twenty thousand Clunkers died in that French battle in March 2008.

The Gremlins

There are some strange human-looking winged gremlins that are very small—one and a half feet tall—that attack gang-handed, 200 or 300 at a time. I never gave them a name, but they're quick and cold and nasty. The faster a being is, the harder it is to tackle. They don't like mustard.

Then there is another being that is very black and tall, with square shoulders and a short neck. It looks human except that instead of a hand, it has a three-pronged claw. I got attacked by one in 1999, and it tore my crown chakra partially off. It took seven years for that wound to heal. My head ached.

Resolution

All evil comes from us humans originally; and it will try to take you toward madness, suicide, violence, and dysfunction. And, certainly, a shaman can help clear those entities from you, but in the end the only way to be rid of them forever is to live a pure life, be kind, and take to the eternal Tao as your companion through life. That is the eventual healing for all our humanity, and we have to wait patiently while people come around to a new way of thinking. There is no other long-term cure.

With the ghouls of whatever kind, always be brave and stand your ground. When you're not scared of them anymore, they eventually go find someone else, as they use the fear they generate as a form of excitement and etheric food.

The light will win in the end, but maybe a hundred billion ghouls have to fall first.

THE WOMEN'S RENEWAL CEREMONY
(GRAY SPERM, WHITE SPERM)

Gray sperm is sperm from men who didn't love you, had no respect for you, or had a silent hatred and disdain for women or a violence toward humanity. Essentially, it's the sperm of a dark soul, acid sperm. It can make you sick.

The sperm of a man who is tender and warm in his care for you, one who has respect for the feminine principle is pure white—literally, in its physical manifestation; and spiritually it is also pure white. It is alkaline sperm. If a man's sperm is yellow, it usually has to do with meat eating and fat in his diet; then his sperm looks like pus.

I feel that it's very helpful for women on the spiritual path to clear out the memory of gray sperm, its trace. But before I explain how that is done, let me give you an understanding of the woman's contribution to gray sperm, for she has a part in it as well.

When a woman degrades her femininity by offering herself to many men or those of low energy—or if she does so in order to help with her security issues, if she accepts money, or if she offers herself to a powerful man she doesn't love in order to elevate her status and lifestyle—she contributes to the acidity of the sperm, its gray color.

When she accepts a partner because she feels ugly inside, or when she is lonely and has sex just to feel whole and momentarily accepted, or if she has casual sex with strangers just for the adrenalin rush, that is also gray and acid. So there are many ways in which she contributes—it's not just the man's disrespect; it's also *her* disrespect for the femininity within her.

If she comes together with a partner she knows and respects, if he has the same love and respect for her, and if he understands energy at a higher level, then a bond of fused energy can be made from the union. Each has to dedicate their orgasm and their love to a higher purpose; then that energy is transmuted to a higher level.

The dedication the two make before lovemaking can be assigned to healing, the family's well-being, or the advancement and perception of each involved . . . many things—whatever both agree to. And sometimes the dedication can serve to allow energy to flow into the 9-D world to be used in ways that are mostly beyond our ken for now. I should say that it's useful but not vital if the chosen dedication is on each person's mind at the time of orgasm—even if that thought is ever so fleeting at that time—and I'd also like to add that it's not necessary for the two orgasms to be simultaneous for the union to be successful.

The dedication ceremony before the union should be short and simple and not laced with pomposities, grand statements, and much ado. It can be nothing more than one partner saying, "Let us dedicate this act to our child's upcoming exams," and both partners agree to that. Keep it brief and simple; there are more pressing matter at hand.

These are very esoteric things, and there are ramifications here. Suffice it to say that these ideas shouldn't be offered to others casually, to a partner who wouldn't understand them and might get angry, or to those who haven't processed their dark side and fail to understand the spiritual journey. It could possibly backfire, as the ghouls can ride the orgasm, and then the sex act would become like black magic.

It's never good to provide heat to the ghouls, empowering them. Heat starvation is one of the main antighoul tactics. One doesn't ever want to offer the heat of negative emotions, sexuality, or deviant acts, as that only brings the ghouls around for dinner, gang-handed.

The Renewal Ceremony

The Renewal Ceremony, where a female wants to make herself whole and release the memory of gray sperm and past lovers, is usually performed together with other women, but it can be done on one's own. I'll give you the simple outline of how it's done in the company of others, and then I'll explain how it can be expanded by you.

1. Fast for three days, and wear nothing but white clothes and undergarments (shoes can be colored). You may drink fruit or vegetable juice or clear vegetable broth. If you don't have time, a one-day fast is fine.

2. During this time, ponder your feminine qualities and review what went right and what went wrong with whichever partner(s) you feel didn't have the ideals and respect of a superior man. In this way you know what it is that you're seeking to release. And of course, reflect on *your* contribution to it.

3. Take time to walk in nature and to ponder the vastness of the feminine spirit, her silent power and grace; and pray to the Goddess for forgiveness, redemption, and resolution.

After the fast, the women's ceremony begins. It's always performed in daylight hours, never at night (important). It is usually held at a sweat lodge, a spa that has private areas and steam rooms, or a private home. The room should be made beautiful with flowers, decorations, and soft music. My old house in Australia had a Japanese bathhouse with steam rooms, showers, a cold-plunge pool, and a tatami room, so it was perfect for women to use for this ceremony.

The women should come in a humble way, dressed in white, with no makeup or jewelry; those things can be placed in their bags for later. The ceremony starts with the lighting of many candles and incense and each woman talking briefly about her life and whatever she wants to say about her feelings. Then there is a short ten-minute process of contemplation that is very important and special. Each woman disrobes from her street clothes, puts a robe or a large towel around herself, and sits facing the wall, with her back to the others. She has a small mirror with her, and she places it in such a way that her lower parts are seen.

Now she contemplates her femininity, the gift of it, and she enters into the domain of her silent power and the presence of the eternal Tao within her. The participants must be silent for this, although soft music may be played if desired. Then she says softly, looking in the mirror, "This is beautiful. I will treasure my femininity and keep it pure, for I am eternal, immortal, universal, and infinite." Each woman can use her own words of love and care to express these sentiments, if she wishes.

The next part is the washing; the steam; and the swimming-pool, plunge-pool, or spa bath—this is usually done in silence or with the women talking in soft voices. The women should wash themselves over and over very vigorously using perfumed cloths. They can help wash each other and help with combing or braiding each other's hair . . . whatever flows from their camaraderie and love for one another.

In the next part of this ceremony, all the women take three vaginal douches each and bless them, saying, "With these I expel the old memories of pain and dysfunction." They use the first douche in private; and then they all come back together and pray, talk, or return to the steam and the showers.

After a while, they do the second douche, cleaning away the old by visualizing and prayer, dismissing and releasing the lovers who disrespected them (or the way *they* disrespected themselves)—people whom they're now finished with or who are unwanted—and those men should be prayed for with love and blessings for their health and good fortune in life.

Then more swimming or steam, or one more shower, and then the final douche.

Next the women anoint their bodies with perfumed oils. Lavender water is also very good. And any of the women can offer massages to one or more of the others if they like the idea.

When the three douches are complete—and by now, of course, many hours will have passed—it is good to offer herb tea and fruit or light snacks, such as pastries that are not too heavy in sugar and cream.

In conclusion, I should say that while I have taught these ideas and the method to maybe a hundred spiritual-warrior women, it goes without saying that I've never actually attended the renewal ceremony, as this is a women's thing. Usually one woman acts as the guide or host through the ceremony, and all the others contribute whatever comes from their inner feelings and soul as the time passes. This is how they make the ceremony their own.

The last part of this ceremony closes with each woman stimulating herself to orgasm, pushing that energy out from the vagina back to the celestial with a short, sharp, soft breath. This orgasm acts as the full stop to what has gone on in the past; it is the line in the sand of the woman's new dedication not to falter as she did in the past.

If a participant can't orgasm at that time, she may do so later, provided that she abstains from sex with anyone until that final stop point has been expressed. There should be no sexual activity between the women. I've been told that usually all are in the same room for this last part (sometimes just with a towel or a blanket covering each woman), and it's very strong. But of course, if any participant wants to be more private and go elsewhere, she can choose to do so.

There are no hard-and-fast rules as to how all these components should be performed, but the douches, the steam, the contemplation and prayer, and the camaraderie and love of the women for one another are vital. At the point of orgasm or just after, each woman should say out loud, but whispered or in a quiet voice, words such as:

*"I am the living spirit within the embodiment of the
Tao and the feminine principle . . . eternal, immortal
universal, and infinite. I dedicate my femininity to walk
alongside the river of the Tao in love, joy, purity, and grace."*

This prayer can be written, inscribed in calligraphy, or printed on a card to take away. Usually it is customary for the guide or host to give a small gift to each of the women—a flower, a rose crystal, or an inexpensive item of jewelry—as a memento.

After the ceremony is over, there can be a good meal and dancing and celebration or any activity the women wish, or they can all just leave—whatever is preferred.

Additional Notes

Women on their moon cycle should wait and not attend this ceremony until after it's completely over.

I don't know if the orgasm dedication mentioned in the preceding section works for gay females—if the union combines and goes on to 9-D or not. I think that it does if there is true love between them. But I am almost 99.99 percent certain that it doesn't work for gay males, as the yin feminine is missing.

All I can say to those who are gay is that they should experiment with the dedication and their love and see what comes of the visions that follow from the love they have expressed for their partners.

237

Thank you. I hope this book has been informative and worthwhile and that you have seen the way to go. If you take to purity and the Three Graces, your evolution is assured.

(**Note from Stuart:** As mentioned previously, this is by my friend Khris Krepcik, whom I consider to be one of the world's experts on the input/output carrier signals, the fractal cube, and the downloads.)

THE MATRIX AND THE HUMAN SOUL

by Khris Krepcik

We know from looking into the Aluna mirror-world that the Matrix exists as an energy field—fields within fields, really. It's a complex holographic program of information bent on controlling the human race. There are vast amounts of information running through it. It contains a vibrational energy pattern for every law, rule, regulation, and negative human sentiment, as well as all of the control mechanisms that we see in the outer world. It also contains entities, thoughtforms, and transdimensional beings that don't want you to break free.

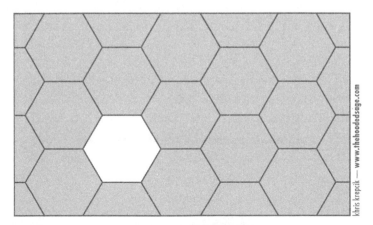

khris krepcik — www.thehoodedsage.com

The Matrix — A Hole in the Grid

When you peer into the Aluna, the Matrix often looks like a honeycomb net or energy grid that you can't get past. But there are openings in it that you can find. To locate a hole in the grid, you have to decide to go the opposite direction from the mind-set and programming of society. Then work to become disciplined; align to nature; and incorporate tender, loving sentiments into the resonance of your soul. And, as Stuart Wilde says, you have to move sideways, becoming wider in your energy and feelings.

Let me explain. What you really are is a multidimensional being. The current existence that you know to be you, your current incarnation as a human being, also exists in the mirror-world as a hyper-dimensional fractal cube of information. Everything about you is in that cube; it's one aspect of your soul connected to an even larger energy, like a bead on a thread of flowing energy.

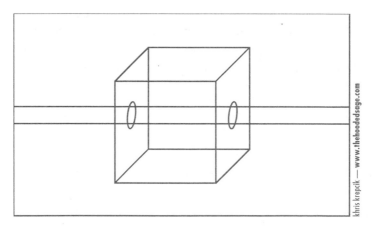

The Human Incarnation — A Hyperdimensional Cube

240

One side of the hypercube you is the holographic program of your ego . . . your identity in the physical plane. I call it your input/output carrier signal, based on the same concept in the *Matrix* movie, where they first locate Neo's position in the real world. When you're rigid in your opinions, the cube doesn't move. It locks you into a certain location in your feelings.

If you've ever felt stuck at a certain point in your journey that you just can't seem to get past, it's because the cube isn't riding the flow of the Eternal Tao. To move sideways and align to the Tao, you have to disrupt your input/output carrier signal, breaking free from its rigid grip. How do you do that? This leads us back to finding a deeper understanding of the Matrix and what it really is.

At one of Mr. Wilde's "See the Morph" events in Amsterdam, I was in a room with eight other people in a very deep trance state. As the Morph set in, the ceiling, floor, and walls all went very hazy and then disappeared. Deeper and deeper into the Morph, the physical appearance of the other people in the room also went nonsolid. They morphed into different energies and combinations of light and form. Eventually, they totally disappeared. But what I noticed was that in each location where a person had previously been, sitting there was now a complex Light Being in their place, like colorful universes hovering in hyperspace.

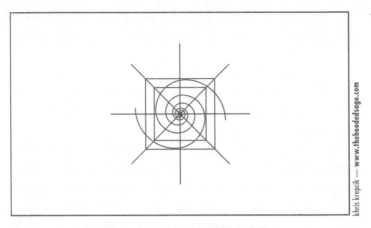

khris krepcik — www.thehoodedsage.com

The Human Soul — A Complex Light Being

It was fascinating to observe. I realized that I was now looking at the inner universe of each of those people, their true souls. Each was a bit different from the next, but every one was a swirling universe of its own.

But it was also quite frightening. I had gone so deep into those worlds that nothing was recognizable from a human perspective, and I wasn't sure if I'd be able to make it back into *this* world. There's really nothing human about the human soul and the dimension it dwells in. It was like leaving 3-D and traversing the Morph worlds into a 26-dimensional one.

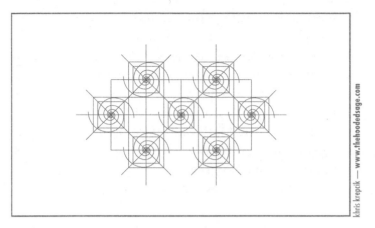

khris krepcik — www.thehoodedsage.com

The Matrix — A Grid of Human Souls

Watching these Light Beings hovering together, I could see lines of energy that connected them all together, forming a complex holographic grid. You could clearly see how the energy from one being would enter into and affect that of another, back and forth between them all: a constant exchange of energy . . . downloads of information.

Rotating back into 3-D, each Light Being morphed back into the 3-D forms as the people I knew them to be. Then it was like my vision would blip back and forth between seeing 3-D and 9-D. At times, you could see the silhouette of their human form, while also seeing their Light Being form as an overlay. Other times, you could see their fractal hypercube hovering around them. I say "around" them, but it's more like it's around them and within them at the same time. The hypercube and inner universe is deep inside, projecting and expanding out beyond the confinement of our physical size.

What is the Matrix? Humans form the Matrix. In the Aluna, it is a complex, nonphysical energy grid of information that is transferred to and from humans. It's the sentiments, desires, and impulses of humans. In the outer world, the Matrix is a manifestation of those inner energies in the form of attitudes, religions, beliefs, governments, and endless systems of control.

The Matrix is the energy grid that connects humankind together. That's not necessarily a bad thing. The problem is that the Matrix has become infested by the darkness of humanity, like a virus program has overwritten the natural program.

The Etheric Tubes and Energy Transference

If you watch the etheric energy that surrounds people in 3-D, you can learn to see the etheric tubes that connect between them. Information transfers from one person to the next. We are constantly projecting and absorbing energy. It looks like little light pellets traveling through a translucent tube. When a person is full of darkness, disdain, negative emotions, greed, and so forth, those pellets look like brown or greenish brown blobs. When a person is genuinely kind and loving and is projecting pure sentiments, the light pellets appear as translucent white or bright colors.

The downloads are fractal codes within the Matrix. They each have a certain resonance, a vibrational energy pattern that enters your etheric hypercube, aligning to or disrupting the resonance you already have inside your soul. Most of the codes in the Matrix are designed to keep you under its control, its prisoner. In the physical plane, they're also delivered to you through your sensory perceptions: taste, touch, smell, sight, and hearing.

The control codes are everywhere. We're constantly bombarded with them. The obvious is in the form of the nightly news, drip feeding the resonance of fear. Advertising, misinformation, music, art, Internet, on and on—and of course, through each other on a personal level—all delivering dark resonances. It seems endless. These control programs work to lock your hypercube in place. Keeping you where you're at.

Understanding how all this works is a major step in learning to break free. First, it should show you just how important it is to clean up your act, process your shadow, and not project your stuff onto others. Second, it shows you a way to defend yourself against the dark influence of others, not allowing them to latch on for a free lunch. This leads us back to disrupting your input/output carrier signal. . . .

Fortunately, there are also programs designed to help you go the other way. We call them hidden trip codes, because they unlock something in your hypercube, something that resonates in your soul. You may not always be able to put your finger exactly on where or what a trip code was, but you feel its effect, as it resonates within. Something inside of you changes. The more trip codes you unlock, the freer your hypercube becomes, allowing your energy to move sideways.

There are powerful trip codes that I've come across in the writings of Stuart Wilde. The secrets to entering these deep inner worlds are all there, hidden in his works but definitely there. The interesting thing is that the codes *had* to be hidden. It's part of keeping access to the celestial doorway safe. It's all very technical in the way it's done. Stuart Wilde told me that he knew some of the codes were there, since he wrote them deliberately, but he didn't know *all* the codes in his books and music, as many are so far beyond what any of us know. He entered some of them without consciously knowing he had placed them there.

There is a second component to these trip codes that are everywhere. Each one has a hidden resonation. To unlock it, your input/output carrier signal has to be open enough to receive it, while your hypercube must also have a part of the resonation already inside of it. The codes are inside of you.

We're not totally alone in finding our way past the Matrix and its control. There are celestial beings that are working to help you make it. These beings are beyond fascinating in their complexity. Information can download to us from them, in the same way that we download information to each other.

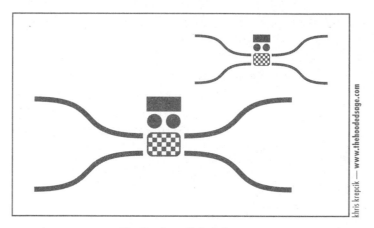

khris krepcik — www.thehoodedsage.com

The Circuitous Light Beings

During one of Mr. Wilde's private events, two of these celestial beings came in and hovered near the group for an hour or so. I call them the Circuitous Light Beings, because their bodies were totally composed of light—light with shape and a digital circuitry that ran throughout their form.

One was a monochromatic golden light, while the other radiated luminous shades of blue. They stretched out across the sky very wide with long, flowing tubes. At their center, where you might call their chest, was a very complex information board. Like a chest plate. It was similar in appearance to a chessboard, only each little square was rotating at high speed, containing video clips, words, images, and symbols. Information would travel through tubes to and from the beings, while the board would retrieve the information, translate it, and then calculate things. At times, the tubes would connect with one of the people attending, and that person would receive a download of information. It was beyond amazing to see.

They always said that one day a force of light would come. . . . I think the Circuitous Beings are the force of light.

Thank you for your time.

— © 2008 Khris Krepcik
www.thehoodedsage.com

ABOUT THE
AUTHOR

Author and lecturer **Stuart Wilde** is an urban mystic, a modern visionary; he has written numerous books on consciousness and awareness, including the very successful Taos Quintet, which are considered classics in their genre. They are: *Miracles, Affirmations, The Force, The Quickening,* and *The Trick to Money Is Having Some!.*

Stuart's perceptive and quirky way of writing has won him a loyal readership over the years. He has a simple way of explaining things that hitherto have seemed a mystery. His books have been translated into 15 languages.

Websites: **www.stuartwilde.com** and
www.redeemersclub.com

Hay House Titles of Related Interest

All of the above are available at your local bookstore, or may be ordered by contacting Hay House (see last page).

We hope you enjoyed this Hay House book. If you'd like to receive a free catalog featuring additional Hay House books and products, or if you'd like information about the Hay Foundation, please contact:

Hay House, Inc.
P.O. Box 5100
Carlsbad, CA 92018-5100

**(760) 431-7695 or (800) 654-5126
(760) 431-6948 (fax) or (800) 650-5115 (fax)
www.hayhouse.com® • www.hayfoundation.org**

Published and distributed in Australia by: Hay House Australia Pty. Ltd., 18/36 Ralph St., Alexandria NSW 2015 • *Phone:* 612-9669-4299 *Fax:* 612-9669-4144 • www.hayhouse.com.au

Published and distributed in the United Kingdom by:
Hay House UK, Ltd., 292B Kensal Rd., London W10 5BE • *Phone:* 44-20-8962-1230 • *Fax:* 44-20-8962-1239 • www.hayhouse.co.uk

Published and distributed in the Republic of South Africa by:
Hay House SA (Pty), Ltd., P.O. Box 990, Witkoppen 2068 • *Phone/Fax:* 27-11-467-8904 • orders@psdprom.co.za • www.hayhouse.co.za

Published in India by: Hay House Publishers India, Muskaan Complex, Plot No. 3, B-2, Vasant Kunj, New Delhi 110 070 • *Phone:* 91-11-4176-1620 • *Fax:* 91-11-4176-1630 • www.hayhouse.co.in

Distributed in Canada by: Raincoast, 9050 Shaughnessy St., Vancouver, B.C. V6P 6E5 • *Phone:* (604) 323-7100 *Fax:* (604) 323-2600 • www.raincoast.com

Tune in to **HayHouseRadio.com®** for the best in inspirational talk radio featuring top Hay House authors! And, sign up via the Hay House USA Website to receive the Hay House online newsletter and stay informed about what's going on with your favorite authors. You'll receive bimonthly announcements about Discounts and Offers, Special Events, Product Highlights, Free Excerpts, Giveaways, and more! **www.hayhouse.com®**